Demystifying the Prophetic: Prophetic Activation

Russell Walden

Copyright © 2014 Russell Walden

All rights reserved.

ISBN: 1497485010
ISBN-13: 9781497485013

DEDICATION

To my dear wife Kitty. Without you, this book would not have been written.

CONTENTS

	Acknowledgments	i
1	Simplicity of the Prophetic	1
2	Fluency in the Prophetic	17
3	Receiving a Group Word	30
4	Prophesying to a Range of People	38
5	The Visionary Response	45
6	The Acoustic Response	55
7	The Perceptive Response	62
8	Ministering from a Pure Stream	68
9	Rightly Discerning What You Hear	78
10	Prophetic Evangelism: Jerusalem	87
11	Public Prophetic Demonstration	97
12	Mentoring in the Prophetic	103

ACKNOWLEDGMENTS

With gratitude I acknowledge the thousands of people I have been privileged to prophesy to over the years. With your cooperation and patience the gifts of God in my life were honed and clarified. May you receive the reward of your service and support of Father's Heart Ministry.

CHAPTER ONE: SIMPLICITY OF THE PROPHETIC

Introduction: The Simplicity of the Prophetic

THE BIRTH OF A PROPHETIC MINISTRY:

I was standing at a lectern relating to a group of people an experience of hearing God's voice. Abruptly from the crowd I was rudely interrupted:

> "That's the problem I have with guys like you... You are always claiming 'God told me!' God never talks to me like that, I just don't accept it. God can't be telling you everything..."

I stared back at the man silently, unsure what to do next. It was 1988 and I was speaking to a group of about 70 pastors and their wives at a monthly minister's luncheon. The host was a good friend of mine who had been leading this group for many years. The crowd seated before me represented denominational pastors as well as independent ministers, all who subscribed in their doctrine to "charismatic" truth and the Holy Spirit led life. I was the young upstart so my response to the challenge would have significant consequences for me.

The pastor who had interrupted me held the pulpit of a large, successful full gospel church in this moderate sized city in the Deep South. His rude objection to my off-handed remark was met with murmurs of approval across the room. What had I said to provoke such an outburst?

To illustrate my message to my fellow pastors that day I had referred to something the Father had said to me, prefacing my remark with *"The Father told me the other day..."*

After loudly interrupting me with his words of ridicule, my well dressed provocateur leaned back in his seat with a self satisfied look on his face, acknowledging the tacit approval of many in the room, who all seemed to agree that *"God just didn't talk to people like that anymore..."*

Usually I'm not very fast on my feet with a "quick come-back". Under normal circumstances I would have mumbled an apology, finished my message and made a hasty exit after the meeting. Today was different. I felt the fire of the Holy Spirit flash from my feet to my chest and I shot back in a strong clear tone:

> *"You mean to tell me that you are NOT on speaking terms with your Father?"*

The pastor hesitated, looking around. The smirk on his face slowly faded to something more like embarrassed anger. I continued, addressing the group:

> *"Are we saying that the norm for Spirit-filled believers is to NOT hear the voice of God, and anyone who DOES is considered an ODDITY?"*

Needless to say I didn't get invited to speak to that well heeled group of pastors very often after that. Driving home that afternoon to the small rural church I had pastored for nearly a decade, I determined in my heart that the people I pastored would be trained in hearing the voice of God with clarity and activated in speaking the Father's words to those who couldn't hear for themselves.

GOD HAS A VOICE, HE WILL NOT LEAVE YOU WITHOUT ANSWERS FOR YOUR LIFE:

The simplicity of the prophetic is found in this definition: *hearing God's voice and articulating what you hear to others*. Not everyone is a prophet, or called to the "five-fold" ministry of a prophet (Eph. 4:11). Prophetic gifting is *available to all* believers in some measure great or small. Every believer is intended by God to know His voice and communicate His voice to others.

God is speaking, whether you hear Him or not. In this book i will train you to hear the Father in very practical ways, and i will challenge you to share what you hear for the benefit of others. Each chapter will have an activation which will require action on your part as you learn to hear the Father's voice with clarity.

Bear in mind that the Kingdom of God doesn't come with observation (Luke 17:20,21). The Kingdom only comes in your life as a participatory act initiated by you and endorsed by positive results through the hand of God. If you only read this material in a casual way it will not be very helpful. You must act and do in order to take full advantage of what the Father has for you in the prophetic.

WHY SHOULD WE TEACH PEOPLE TO HEAR THE VOICE OF GOD?

Eph. 4:11 - 12 says that the Apostle, Prophet, Evangelist, Pastor and Teacher are in the body of Christ not just to HEAR GOD FOR YOU but *to train you also how to hear God for yourself*. God's intention is for you to walk out your own personal destiny and ministry portion. In other words, our job is to work ourselves out of a job by training, instructing and mentoring you till you hear the Father's voice with clarity and are activated and empowered to bring the kingdom of God to bear in your life and the lives of others.

DEMONSTRATION OF THE SPIRIT AND OF POWER:
(1 Corinthians 2:4) And my speech and my preaching [was] not with enticing words of man's wisdom, but in demonstration of the Spirit and of power:

Paul knew the futility of mere words. It isn't enough to merely talk ABOUT GOD. When you are sharing Christ, what you are successful in talking someone INTO, someone else will come along and be successful in talking them OUT OF. Paul knew this and didn't bother trying to TALK people INTO accepting Christ. He simply DEMONSTRATED Christ first hand in SPIRIT and in POWER. In so doing Paul's audience was FORCED to make a decision having been confronted directly with the SPIRIT of God and the POWER of GOD.

There are two ways to walk in demonstration:

1. You can demonstrate the SPIRIT (through the prophetic, prophecy, word of knowledge, word of wisdom, tongues and interpretation.).

2. You can demonstrate the POWER (through healing, casting out devils, miracles, raising the dead, etc.).

The demonstration of the SPIRIT is meant to BRING the demonstration of power. Example: When John the Baptist came, the scriptures tell us, *"John did no miracle..."* (See John 10:41). Yet, though he did no mighty acts, John nonetheless ACTIVATED JESUS in His miracle ministry. This demonstrates to us that the PROPHETIC activates the CHRIST IN YOU, which is the hope of God's Glory in your life (See Col. 1:25-27).

If you look in the scriptures you will see that Jesus didn't do any miracles until John by the spirit of prophecy activated the CHRIST CALLING on the INSIDE OF HIM according to the Father's plan. So John who did no miracle activated Jesus in His miracle ministry. This is the essential role of the prophet where the people of God are concerned. The prophet's job is to activate who Jesus is in your life toward the end of launching you into your ministry purpose.

This is the calling and commission of every prophet, and the ultimate and underlying purpose of every prophetic gifting or utterance: *TO SPEAK TO THE CHRIST IN YOU ...*

John knew he wasn't worthy to loose the sandal strap of the Christ that was in Jesus (John 1:27). He was a prophet like none before him or since but he knew his place, as you should know yours if you are going to accept the privilege of speaking the Father's voice to His children.

Being a prophet or moving in the prophetic is about SPEAKING to the CHRIST in every believer and ACTIVATING who Jesus DIED TO BE ON THE INSIDE OF THEM. There is no place for an aloof, elitist attitude in the prophetic.

So be encouraged to absorb this material and do the activations, for there is much reward and great enjoyment in being used of God in this way.

ACTIVATING THE GIFTS OF GOD IN YOUR LIFE:

Each chapter of this book will present an aspect of the prophetic geared to challenge your faith and build you up in the gifting that God has imparted uniquely to you. Again, with each chapter there will be an ACTIVATION. Remember that the kingdom of God does not come to the mere observer. You must be a participator if you want to see the anointing and blessing of God in your life in any area.

Bear in mind that from the perspective of our discipline method you can't make a mistake or "do it wrong." Just relax, and allow the Holy Spirit to lead you from where you are into greater fluency of all nine of the gifts of the Spirit (See 1 Cor.12:1-20).

> *PLEASE NOTE: The baseline assumption for this material is that you have accepted Christ as your savior, and have experienced the new birth.*

THE ACTIVATION PROCESS:

To begin, a little orientation is in order for understanding the activation process. The activations each week will be different and unique but the approach will remain much the same.

What exactly IS a prophetic activation?

Prophetic Activation is the means by which we identify the various ways in which God speaks to you and then attempt to open you up to be used in that particular manner. It is about challenging yourself and stretching yourself by yielding to God through the operation of the gifts of the Holy Spirit.

REMEMBER: THE GIFTS OF THE SPIRIT ARE NOT MERIT BADGES:

The prophetic gifts or the other gifts of the Spirit for that matter are not MERIT BADGES. They are *charisms* or *grace-lets* as the original language of the scriptures tell us. That which comes by grace is not based on your maturity, holiness or merit. You can't be good enough. You just have to *make yourself available* to be used by the Holy Spirit.

Trust in God to guide you through this material, rely on Him and don't let yourself be condemned into thinking God won't use you. After all, God spoke through a braying ass once, why wouldn't He use the worst of us (See 2 Peter 2:16)?

Another way of saying this is that God gives us His ability as an unearned gift even when you don't deserve it. It is not something you work for but is a free gift activated by releasing your FAITH. In addition, you don't have to FEEL anything in particular in order to be used in the Gifts of the Spirit (although you may experience great spasms of emotion when you prophesy which is perfectly fine). The only prerequisite is accepting the truth of the gifts of God and releasing your faith and stepping out.

So again, you:

1. See the truth of the gifts of God.

2. Accept that the gifting is available without merit by grace.

3. Step out in faith and give what you best feel and sense God is giving you.

These three steps comprise the activation process i will take you through in each assignment. Learning to move in the prophetic or any of the other gifts is not some deep secret. It simply involves the same transaction of faith by which you came to accept Jesus as your savior in the first place:

THE SIMPLICITY OF GAINING FLUENCY IN THE PROPHETIC GIFTS:

Here is an example of how the prophetic works similiar receiving the new birth experience:

1. At some point in your life you heard the message of the Gospel that Jesus died to save you from yourself and bring you by the new birth into the family of God.

2. The Holy Spirit moved on your heart and mind and you became convinced that what you were hearing was truth and from God himself.

3. You realized that God didn't expect you to be "good enough" to receive his gift of salvation and you chose to accept His unmerited favor.

4. You went beyond just *hearing* and *acted* upon the truth you are now convinced of and responded in some way by which you prayed to accept Christ as your savior and became in fact born again.

You will learn in this material to move in the Gifts of the Spirit in just this same way. The same way you accepted Christ is very similar to how you allow yourself to be used by God in the gifts of the Spirit. This is true specifically when used in the knowledge gifts utilizing the same principles by which you came to accept Christ in the first place. This is because you GROW IN GOD in any area of gifting in the same way you came to be BORN INTO HIS KINGDOM IN THE FIRST PLACE.

This is the simple, child-like truth of operating in spiritual gifts. There are no "trade secrets" or "hidden revelations". In this material we are demystifying the prophetic. God has a voice. He wants to be heard. He wants you to share what you heard with His help to touch the lives of others for the Kingdom.

THERE ARE THREE GIFTS THAT COMPLEMENT AND COMPRISE PROPHETIC GIFTING:

Throughout this material you will be developing fluency in three of the nine gifts of the Spirit:

1. Prophecy

2. Word of knowledge

3. Word of wisdom

These are the gifts that are primarily in use when someone prophesies. These activations will also be helpful with the other seven gifts of the Spirit, activating the gifts of tongues, interpretation of tongues, discerning of spirits, faith, healing and miracles because they are all developed in like manner.

These gifts are different from each other but the process is essentially the same. Once you become familiar with the activation process i will teach you, fluency in all the gifts will come much easier.

The purpose of each activation is to stretch you and draw out your spiritual gifts in a safe, loving environment. You can't make a mistake and no one is going to tell you that you 'did it wrong'.

WHAT IS THE SCRIPTURAL BASIS FOR MOVING IN THE PROPHETIC AND THE GIFTS OF THE SPIRIT?

Let's consider a few more scriptures:

> *(1 Corinthians 12:1) Now concerning spiritual [gifts], brethren, I would not have you ignorant.*

Over 100 years have passed since Pentecostal/Charismatic experience was restored to God's people through the Azusa Street Revival in Los Angeles. Yet there is still much ignorance, superstition and resistance to the gifts of God. One lady I know reports that in her country to identify your gifting in the prophetic is virtual "Christian suicide".

So prepare yourself as you learn about the prophetic and gain activation in the prophetic gifts, that not everyone will be as thrilled about it as you are. Determine in your heart now that LOVE will be the rule by which you conduct yourself in every transaction, even when you are rejected and rebuffed in your gifting.

> *(1 Corinthians 14:40) Let all things be done decently and in order.*

Many leaders, teaching on the gifts of the Spirit do more to QUENCH the Spirit by emphasizing the "decently and in order" above rather than "let all things be done".

1 Cor. 1:31 tells us *"you may ALL prophesy, that all may learn and all may be comforted."* No matter how staid and traditional your worship service might be, if the gifts of God are not in evidence then that is INDECENT and OUT OF ORDER!

Do you ever go to church and hear someone afterward say, *"I didn't get anything out of that service..."* Well, if we maintained an environment of openness to the Spirit of God and liberty for the people to be used of God then ALL WOULD LEARN AND ALL WOULD BE COMFORTED according to the scriptures (if we actually believed the testimony of scripture!).

In the early church experience we find liberty, order and maturity as all who were moved upon by the Spirit of God were given place to exercise their gifting:

> *(1 Corinthians 14:26) How is it then, brethren? when ye come together, every one of you hath a psalm, hath a doctrine, hath a tongue, hath a revelation, hath an interpretation. Let all things be done unto edifying.*

Many leaders criticize these observations but until you get New Testament results and see New Testament power in your community and church then you really aren't in a position to disapprove of New Testament methodology. These practices were given for us to follow and emulate. If we fail to do so then we as leaders fall short of our calling.

In the prophetic i want to encourage and nurture you to hear His voice and share it with others. You will be amazed at the accuracy and timeliness of the most innocuous things that you might think don't amount to much, but in fact completely change the lives of your targeted hearers.

DEVELOPING THE GIFTS: CAN YOU LEARN HOW TO PROPHESY?:

(Hebrews 5:14) But strong meat belongeth to them that are of full age, [even] those who by reason of use have their senses exercised to discern both good and evil.

The gifts of the Spirit don't emerge in your life fully formed. They develop in you like a language. Over time and practice you become fluent in the gifts of the Spirit. The anointing increases as you connect with those who have a greater experience and mantle of anointing than you are walking in at the time.

As you exercise your gifting, you will learn how to flow and release yourself in the Spirit of God. You will also learn how not to quench the Spirit or grieve Him by succumbing to other influences. You learn by doing. The kingdom of God doesn't come with observation, it comes through active participation.

EDIFICATION, EXHORTATION, AND COMFORT:

(1 Corinthians 12:7) But the manifestation of the Spirit is given to every man to profit withal.

> *(1 Corinthians 14:3) But he that prophesieth speaketh unto men [to] edification, and exhortation, and comfort.*

Much harm has come to the prophetic movement through immature and misinformed leaders who speak curses, pronounce judgments speak rebuke, and reproof in the context of *"thus saith the Lord..."*

Most teachers in the prophetic today will claim that the average layman who prophesies has no right to do anything but *"edify, exhort, and comfort"*. However they go on to assert and claim that the man or woman *"in the office"* of a prophet allegedly has authority to condemn, judge, rebuke and reprove. There is no New Testament precedent for this in the prophetic.

Whether you are called to the OFFICE OF A PROPHET or simply aspire to the prophetic as a believer, there is no *"license to kill"* no *"007"* anointing. You can extensively study the life of every New Testament prophet and you won't find ONE that operated outside the parameters of *"edification, exhortation, and comfort"*.

When you receiving a *"word"* from a prophet, if that prophet steps over into condemnation and judgment, you are under no compunction from the Father to accept that as His word. There are times it is true that the Father will rebuke and correct quite vociferously, but the prophetic is not the tool or instrument through which that judgment will come. This misdirected idea of the prophetic arises from an Old Testament paradigm as opposed to New Testament practice.

ALL MAY PROPHESY:
(1 Corinthians 14:31) For ye may all prophesy one by one, that all may learn, and all may be comforted.

All born again, Spirit filled believers have the nine gifts of the Spirit available to them but some will demonstrate more enablement than others. God has imparted the gifts to His children, yet He still divides and distributes to individuals as He wills based on desire, calling and ability to receive and step out. So to develop your gifting to the full, this material will provoke you to step up, step out and give out to the fullest measure of that sample of prophetic gifting the Father has imparted specifically to you.

Chapter One Assignment:

ACTIVATION: PROPHETIC PRAYING

Remember that Luke 17:20,21 tell us that the kingdom of God doesn't come with observation. You have to do something. Here is your assignment for chapter one:

Choose five people in your life to pray for. Don't feel compelled to come out with a "thus saith the Lord." It isn't even necessary for you to share what God gives you with them if you are not comfortable doing so. This activation is very low key intended to just get you comfortable with the idea of praying for others in a prophetic context.

The scripture tells us with each gift there are differences of administration (1 Cor. 12:5). We can compare this to medicine. You can take medicine in a pill, a patch, an injection, and so on. Likewise the prophetic word doesn't apply or come forth through you in just one way. In fact depending on the setting YOU GET TO CHOOSE because *"the spirit of the prophet is subject to the prophet"* (See 1 Cor. 14:32).

WHAT IS PROPHETIC PRAYING AND HOW DOES IT WORK?:

Prophetic praying is a way to prophesy that involves yielding to the Holy Spirit as you pray for someone. You will simply relax into the flow of the anointing and trust the Holy Ghost to give you the words, the thoughts and expressions that cause your prayer to become more than the sum total of its parts and truly bless the person you pray over (your target or recipient).

The end result of prophetic praying leaves the subject of your praying knowing that God spoke to him or her directly as you *"prayed out the mysteries of God"* over them. In this prayer, the gift of prophecy, word of knowledge and word of wisdom will all make themselves evident though you may not realize it at the time. Don't try too hard. Just pray out your heart toward that person. Put it in writing, in an e-mail or record it into a recorder to perhaps share later.

This is a good method for prophesying over someone who doesn't know about the prophetic. It doesn't matter what you call it, if the Holy Spirit breathes through you into that person's life in your prayer and that is all that matters.

If you are in a classroom setting then pair off in the group with someone you don't know to do this exercise.

THE PURPOSE OF THE "PROPHETIC PRAYING" ACTIVATION:

When you exercise prophetic praying you will activate in yourself sensitivity to the voice of the Holy Spirit. The beauty of this activation is that it flows in the familiar format of prayer that any believer will be comfortable with. The goal is to relax. Don't worry about speaking in the first person or saying, *"thus saith the Lord..."* Forget about style of delivery and just pray out of your heart by the leading of the Holy Spirit as best you can.

STEP BY STEP WALK THROUGH OF THE "PROPHETIC PRAYING ACTIVATION":

As you pray, realize that the Holy Spirit (Christ in you) will "enter into" your praying without you making any effort whatsoever other than simple yielding of your mind to the natural, restful flow of compassionate prayer for another. You are a born again person. Christ living on the inside of you. Just allow him to minister through you as you pray.

SPIRIT INSPIRED PRAYING:

This activation is very low key. You don't have to conjure up any unnatural intensity or loudness. Just pray out of your heart. The Holy Ghost will enter into your praying and you will be amazed at how accurate and edifying what you share will be.

ACTIVATE YOURSELF AND STEP OUT:

How do we activate ourselves in prophetic praying?

1. Remember that you are one of the ALL who may prophesy according to 1 Cor. 14:31 If *"all may prophesy"* then all (including you) have some level of prophetic gifting. Remember, prophetic gifting in its simplicity is about hearing the Father's voice and sharing it with others.

2. You have a lot of mistakes to make before you get it right. You won't get it right every time. It's ok. You aren't being graded. You are entering into a fluency exercise whereby you will improve with time. You will become more anointed, more accurate and more right on as you step out and give what you have in this safe environment.

3. We are all learners, even someone who has been prophesying for years will tell you that every time you prophesy it's a step of faith and trusting God to lead, guide and instruct you. Relax and share what you have.

PRAY IN THE HOLY GHOST:

Praying in the Spirit or, in tongues connects your volition, your mind and emotions directly to the Holy Spirit to allow His thoughts, impressions, pictures, to come through in your praying. It isn't about external stimulus but an act of faith even if you don't "feel" anything. If you don't pray in tongues don't worry about this part i will help you with that gift later.

I've trained myself and conditioned my spirit man to respond when I ask the Father after praying in the Spirit "what would you say to your servant".

If I get "stuck" I don't stop speaking, I switch over into tongues to break through the "choke point" and continue ministering prophetically.

ACTIVATION PRAYER:
Approximate this prayer as you get ready to do the Activation Assignment:

> *Father, I acknowledge that the Holy Spirit dwells within me. I ask that His thoughts overshadow my merely human intuition as I present my whole body as a living sacrifice you. I bring every thought into captivity to the mind of Christ. I will be open to Jesus my savior as He resides as Christ living within me as I pray. Give me boldness to speak those things you would have me pray. Help me not to doubt or hesitate, but simply release what you are inspiring me to say and pray. Amen.*

NOW GO SILENT AND LISTEN, LOOK AND FEEL:
Relax because this is about having fun. Go "down inside" and open your inner ears and eyes to receive the grace to start off and pray. Give yourself about one minute of silence and look and see what information presents in your mind's eye. Listen to hear and pay close heed starts to "percolate" in your "knower". Remember it's about "seeing, hearing, feeling".

Let's cover these different modes of receiving:

If you are a "seer", you will see pictures in your mind quite spontaneously. These pictures no doubt will need interpretation but make an effort to give exactly what you see in your heart. Interpretation will come later.

If you are a "hearer", the Spirit will come to you in more of an auditory way in the acoustics of your inner man. This will not likely be an audible voice but might be occasionally. It may be more like you are hearing something inwardly. When you think you've heard enough to proceed you simply pray out in your reply what you hear the Spirit saying to you for this assignment.

If God speaks to you in your "knower," you will more or less describe the moving of the Spirit upon you as "feeling after" the voice of the Father. You "just know" what He wants you to say or do. This may even be an actual sensation in your body which would lead you to pray for healing.

PRAY ACCORDING TO THE SPIRIT'S LEADING:

Now it is time to do what we have prepared ourselves to do. Go ahead and pray, speaking or typing or recording ONLY what you feel you are being led to pray by the Holy Spirit. Remember, we are not trying to perform or give formal "thus saith the Lord" prophecy but rather relax and pray a prophetic prayer. As the recipient receives what you share it will register in their heart according to the unction of the Holy Spirit in your praying. Be bold don't hold back - remember you can't make a mistake.

CHAPTER TWO: BASIC GUIDELINES AND FLUENCY IN THE PROPHETIC

HOW TO GIVE A PROPHETIC WORD: FLUENCY IN THE PROPHETIC, PROPHESYING AT WILL:

When you give a prophetic word do you have a choice whether or not you "receive" something?

Can EVERYONE prophesy?

Can you prophesy AT WILL?

There are many and varied opinions about this in the body of Christ. In answer to these questions, let's review the following scriptures:

> *(1 Corinthians 12:7-11) - 7 But the manifestation of the Spirit is given to every man to profit withal. 8 For to one is given by the Spirit the word of wisdom; to another the word of knowledge by the same Spirit; 9 To another faith by the same Spirit; to another the gifts of healing by the same Spirit; 10 To another the working of miracles; to another prophecy; to another discerning of spirits; to another [divers] kinds of tongues; to another the interpretation of tongues: 11 But all these worketh that one and the selfsame Spirit, dividing to every man severally as he will.*

The passage above itemizes what we call "the nine gifts of the spirit". The most commonly used gift is the gift of speaking in other tongues. For the purposes of this material I will assume that you in fact have spoken in tongues and probably do so often. If I were to ask you to pray right now, you could bow your head and pray in your native tongue. If I asked you to then pray "in the spirit" most of you would bow your head and pray in tongues, or the theological term "glossalalia".

You can pray in tongues when you want to can't you? (For myself, since I was baptized in the Holy Spirit in 1972. I find I can pray in tongues at will. I can switch back and forth between my native tongue (English) and the gift of tongues whenever I choose. Is there a scriptural basis for this? (Don't forget to breathe here I am in the process of kicking over a sacred cow). If you can pray in tongues when you wish does it not follow that you can and should operate in all the nine gifts of the spirit AT WILL?

> *(1 Corinthians 14:32) - 32 And the spirits of the prophets are subject to the prophets.*

In the preceding verse Paul was instructing that those exercising spiritual gifts should not interrupt each other or cause disorder in the meeting when they shared their gifting. The insight we gain here is that the person exercising a spiritual gift has control or the initiative to operate in that gift at will.

When I first got my "prayer language" it didn't come easy. When I wanted to pray in tongues I would have to stop and focus, then let the gift find its expression then go ahead and pray in tongues. In other words, in the beginning I wasn't as fluent in speaking in tongues as I am now.

Next question: When you read 1 Cor. 12:7-11 do you see any special designation for the gift of tongues? Is the gift of tongues in some special category whereby it doesn't operate like ALL the other nine gifts of the

Spirit? If you study the scriptures you will find that there is no stated distinction in category or description between the gift of tongues and the other eight gifts mentioned in 1 Cor. 12.

Unfortunately there is a distinction between tongues and the other gifts in our religious culture and tradition, but scripture doesn't validate it. In our religious traditions (whether you are from a Charismatic or a more conservative Pentecostal background) it is customary in practice to regard tongues as a gift we can pretty much operate in at will but that we cannot operate in prophecy, healing, miracles, etc., at will. Again this is a tradition that is not validated by the scripture. So for the purposes of this material I are laying aside that tradition as mere superstition because it doesn't suit the purpose of cultivating the prophetic gifts in your life.

Because you CAN pray in tongues at will, you then DO so according to the level of experience and fluency you have in your "prayer language". This SHOULD apply to ALL the gifts of the Spirit including prophecy.

You can prophesy when you want.

You CAN exercise the gift of healing at will.

You CAN move in miracles at will.

You CAN flow in the gift of discernment, word of knowledge, etc. when you want to, when you need to, when others around you are needing ministry by the Holy Spirit's direction.

If you find this difficult if not impossible it isn't because the scriptures say you can't but because there is a need to cultivate the gifts that God has given you. They are GIFTS by the way. If I give you a shiny new car you don't have to call me every time you want to drive it do you? It's the same way with the gifts of the Spirit. The conclusion then is, with practice and yielding yourself to the Holy Spirit you can prophesy AT will whenever you want, to whoever asks you. This is how I go to a prophetic meeting and prophesy to every person in the room over the course of seven hours and more at a time. The spirit of the prophets is subject to the prophets. This activation material is about helping you gain fluency in the prophetic so that it is available when you need it and when others around you need what God has invested in you.

THE CHARACTER OF THE WORDS YOU GIVE MUST BE SCRIPTURAL:

It is not wrong to pursue or seek to cultivate the gifts of the Spirit in your life. In fact the scriptures tell us to be zealous, motivated, and focused on developing the gifts of God. The most important thing we need to know about prophecy is that it isn't used to beat people up or to speak judgment or correction. The prophecy that comes out in negative, threatening, corrective, or condemnatory tones is a false prophecy at worst or a prophecy contaminated by human character at best. No one, not even someone who sits in the office of a prophet has the authority to speak correction or judgment in the name of the Lord. If you study exhaustively the character of the New Testament prophets you will see that this is true, although it is contrary to the traditions of most churches and so-called prophets. Consider the following scriptures:

> *(1 Corinthians 14:3, 12, 32 KJV) - 3 But he that prophesieth speaketh unto men [to] edification, and exhortation, and comfort. ... 12 Even so ye, forasmuch as ye are zealous of spiritual [gifts], seek that ye may excel to the edifying of the church...*

The scripture above doesn't give any caveat or exception for the office of a prophet. Whether you are a prophet or simply a prophetic believer the constraint you operate under is "edification, exhortation and comfort." Perhaps one of the biggest misconceptions people have of prophetic ministry is that it should be ministered in a judgmental, condemning or in a rebuking way.

Demystifying the Prophetic: Prophetic Activation Internship

Budding prophetic ministries can often fall into the trap of thinking they must come forth with some heavy word of direction or correction in order to somehow lend credence to their position before God and men as a "heavy weight" in the spirit.

The actual fact is that the scripture clearly indicates the primary purpose of prophetic ministry is edification, exhortation and comfort. This means to build up, stir up and to cheer up. NO ONE, NOT EVEN THE "BIG BOY" PROPHETS ARE EXEMPT FROM THIS SIMPLE PROTOCOL. There is no scriptural basis for believing (as is common in prophetic ministry today) that the person in the OFFICE of a PROPHET is exempt from "edification, exhortation, and comfort". These prophets erroneously think they are like a spiritual "007" with a license to "slice and dice" the people of God and tear them down as part of their calling. This is wrong and cannot be supported by New Testament protocols for the prophetic ministry.

The true, mature, internationally recognized prophetic ministries spend a predominate amount of their ministry centered on edification, exhortation and comfort. Mature ministers know that if a correction should be given, it is done in a private, give and take setting. When confrontation is necessary it should never be given in the unilateral, one-sided modality of a "thus saith the Lord".

To prophesy correction behind "thus saith the Lord" is cowardice. If correction is called for, it should come face to face and with an opportunity for dialog, even if it is heated and uncomfortable. It is wrong for a prophet to hide behind "thus saith the Lord".

The New Testament does not legitimize any "thus saith the Lord" prophetic utterance that goes beyond edification, exhortation and comfort. Remember you are a PROPHET OF THE GOSPEL, not a Moses with the stone tablets, hurling them at your hapless victims. Yes, leaders can bring correction, direction, discipline etc., and even creative initiative through their ministry, but the issue is the delivery method. It should be done eye to eye in honest dialog and open communication, not parading in behind an impenetrable shield of "thus saith the Lord". The "thus saith the Lord" mode of delivery is SO powerful that God reserves it for edification, exhortation and comfort.

GIVING DIRECTIVE PROPHECY:

If you read the guidelines taught by many in the prophetic they often say "prophecy is NEVER directive". What they mean by that is that it isn't allowable to say in prophecy "God wants you to do thus and so". However if you read through the scriptures there are many instances of directive words to individuals. In fact most of the prophecies to individuals in the bible you will find were ALMOST ALWAYS directive. So again, we kick over a sacred cow. It is true that prophesying a directive word to an immature believer can be a problem. This is why when we do prophesy we make every effort not only to give the word of the Lord to the person, but to also ACTIVATE THE VOICE OF GOD in their own life and make them responsible to the CHRIST IN THEM not the just the prophetic word from us.

Does God ever call for someone to speak directively? Of course but there is a difference between correction and direction. Strangely enough, those who accept a prophet's rights to call down fire from heaven almost universally say that prophecy should not be directive in character. This again is not supported in the New Testament model for the prophetic ministry.

OLD TESTAMENT VERSUS NEW TESTAMENT PROPHETS:

> *"And if I have the gift of prophecy, and know all mysteries and all knowledge; and if I have all faith, so as to remove mountains, but do not have love, I am nothing." (1Cor. 13:2)*

For the New Testament believer the heart of God is expressed in the life and character of Jesus:

> *(Hebrews 1:1-2 KJV) - 1 God, who at sundry times and in divers manners spake in time past unto the fathers by the prophets, 2 Hath in these last days spoken unto us by [his] Son, whom he*

hath appointed heir of all things, by whom also he made the worlds;

In the past, God spoke in many modalities through the law and the prophets. Now He is speaking through His son Jesus. Did Jesus step on toes or did He wash feet? Did He ever "call down fire" or cancer, or poverty or dire consequences on others? In fact when His followers sought to do this He said:

(Luke 9:54-55 KJV) - 54 And when his disciples James and John saw [this], they said, Lord, wilt thou that we command fire to come down from heaven, and consume them, even as Elias did? 55 But he turned, and rebuked them, and said, Ye know not what manner of spirit ye are of.

So let us in developing our gifts, be diligent to maintain alignment with the character and spirit of Christ when moving in the prophetic gift. Don't deal with people according to their problem deal with them according to their need. This is the redemptive approach.

ADJUST THE EXERCISE OF YOUR GIFT TO THE SETTING WHERE YOU ARE OPERATING:

With different groups there are various guidelines given for moving in the gifts or prophesying to groups or individuals. Home groups tend to be more relaxed, whereas larger churches might want you to ask permission from an elder so what you share can be heard on the P.A. system.

Some churches have an open mike others will not make room for anyone they don't know to give a prophecy. Some churches have a policy of prior approval. It isn't wrong to comply with the guidelines of a ministry that isn't your own to control. You are a guest and you should use common decency and etiquette in all your dealings, particularly the prophetic. The prophetic has a bad name because prophetic people use the excuse of their gift to be rude, obnoxious and insulting. You should at all costs obey the hand of the Spirit on you, but do so with grace and humility even if you are called upon to circumvent to accepted protocol in any given meeting.

It is important to understand that most pastors are usually just trying to be responsible for their flocks. I was a pastor for twenty years and I'm familiar with this tension between wanting the prophetic to be in the group but not wanting to clean up the mess an immature prophet can make. There are always exceptions to this principle. Obey God in all things. We don't discourage "PARKING LOT PROPHECY." Just be mature enough to endure the consequences gracefully if you are corrected.

CORPORATE OR GROUP WORDS ARE DIFFERENT:

Avoid giving directive words to an open congregation, such as "go buy that acreage across town or you have missed God..." This type of corporate directive word should go to the leaders first. Although God may give you a word that would change the entire direction or flow of a service, the responsibility for that decision is ultimately given to the leadership by God and should be channeled through them. DON'T be offended if your word is held back.

ACCEPT THE FACT THAT YOUR WORD IS SUBJECT TO SCRUTINY:

Always ask an individual "May I give you a word?" before you prophesy. Just because you "have a word" doesn't mean the intended target has no choice but to hear it. They have the right to decline. If that happens, don't be offended. Just smile and say thanks and move on. This is a cardinal, universal rule in the prophetic.

Be willing always to have a word judged. If the nature of the word is a personal prophecy a good policy is to have a witness with you, or to in some way record what is spoken. (digital voice recorders, written out words, etc.)

> *(1 Corinthians 14:29 KJV) - 29 Let the prophets speak two or three, and let the other judge.*

Don't be intimidated by scrutiny. Prophetic words are so powerful and so overwhelming at times that the Father gives the recipients the right and the authority to judge the word and accept it or reject it. They won't always do it right and they will reject you at times but you can't afford to be childish or get offended. Just move on. You've done your job.

VERBAGE, LANGUAGE AND DELIVERY:
Avoid unless specifically directed by the spirit "religious" mannerisms such as 16th century English, etc. Give the word in your natural, conversational vocabulary.

HOW TO RECEIVE A WORD:
STAY OPEN:
Even in the early church the prophetic and personal prophesy was not widely accepted or without controversy. Paul taught his constituents:

> *(1 Thessalonians 5:20 KJV) - 20 Despise not prophesyings.*

There are many reasons for despising a prophecy. They might fail to come to pass. Someone who is not experienced in the prophetic might do a poor job of ministering to you. An immature person might speak harshly over you "in the name of the Lord". Even a seasoned prophet might speak over you a prophecy that doesn't come to pass.

Stay open. Stay humble. Be flexible and forgiving. Blessed are the flexible, they don't get bent out of shape.

JUDGE THE WORD:
Does the word come from a reputable source? That is a tricky one because of the following verse:

> *(2 Peter 2:16 KJV) - 16 But was rebuked for his iniquity: the dumb ass speaking with man's voice forbad the madness of the prophet.*

Sometimes God uses unlikely messengers to speak the word of the Lord. As for me I often pray, "God, I just want to be the ass that the Lord rides in on!"

DOES THE WORD GIVEN STAND UP TO SCRIPTURAL PRINCIPLES AND TRUTHS?

This is an important consideration. However, always remember that although a word might contradict your understanding of the scripture, that doesn't mean it truly, contradicts scripture. It has been rightly said "truth heard the first time almost always produces a negative reaction".

DOES THE WORD "BEAR WITNESS TO YOUR SPIRIT"?

(Isaiah 55:12 KJV) - 12 For ye shall go out with joy, and be led forth with peace...

That doesn't mean the word is false, but that you should wait for confirmation that gives you the assurance you have heard from the Father.

PROPHESY IS ALMOST ALWAYS CONDITIONAL:

All the promises of God are conditional including prophetic promises, whether stated or not. You should write your prophecy out. You should consider what the prophesy is calling upon you to do. Prophecies are conditional upon factors such as faith, obedience, timing, etc. are very important. Most prophesies fail because the recipient didn't acknowledge, accept or act on the conditions specified in the word.

COOPERATE WITH THE PROPHETIC WORD AS MUCH AS POSSIBLE:

If it is determined that a word is from God, several things can be done to cooperate with God in the fulfillment of the word.

MIX THE WORD WITH FAITH:

> *(Hebrews 4:2 KJV) - 2 For unto us was the gospel preached, as well as unto them: but the word preached did not profit them, not being mixed with faith in them that heard [it].*

War a good warfare with your prophecy: Write the word out, confess it, declare it, remind yourself, your enemy and God himself about the word on a regular basis.

> *(1 Timothy 1:18 KJV) - 18 This charge I commit unto thee, son Timothy, according to the prophecies which went before on thee, that thou by them mightest war a good warfare;*

Understand about the issue of prophetic timing: Remember prophetic words are PAST, PRESENT AND FUTURE. So don't discount a word that deals with the past in the present tense. Be patient also for the timing of the promise as it unfolds in days, monthly perhaps many years:

> *(Psalm 105:19 KJV) - 19 Until the time that his (Joseph's) word came: the word of the LORD tried him.*

BOUNDARIES OF THIS TRAINING ENVIRONMENT:

There are do's and don'ts for the prophetic activations that we will suggest in this material. If you are studying this individually or with a group, consider the following:

Use wisdom: Do not make any major life or directive decisions based on words given in this training environment. People with different levels of giftedness will prophesy to you. As with any prophecy, wait for unquestioned confirmation from multiple sources before acting on any directive word.

> *(1 Corinthians 14:29 KJV) - 29 Let the prophets speak two or three, and let the other judge.*

> *(2 Corinthians 13:1 KJV) - 1 This [is] the third [time] I am coming to you. In the mouth of two or three witnesses shall every word be established.*

DON'T BE A PROPHETIC LITTLE NAPOLEON:
Don't demand that others accept the words given about your calling or giftedness: Don't get a word about what a good guy you are and then harass your spouse about it next time you argue. Don't say, "see God SAID I was right...." That isn't very mature is it?

Do not use words identifying your call or your giftedness to pressure others to agree or cooperate with how you want to exercise that call.

DON'T BE PUSHY:
Again, always ask if possible, "May I give you a word?" It is ok if someone says, "Thanks but no thanks!"

Offer words to recipients with humility. All of us, even the most mature have to filter what we give through our human personality.

> *(1 Corinthians 13:12 KJV) - 12 For now we see through a glass, darkly; but then face to face: now I know in part; but then shall I know even as also I am known.*

Do not become offended if a trainee "misses it" on something, offered to you. Let the children play. Don't be unwilling to be a guinea pig!

THERE IS NO PASS OR FAIL IN THIS MATERIAL:
We want to clarify that this material is not about "pass or fail". The intention is that we will learn and grow together in the prophetic. I are here to ACTIVATE YOUR GIFTING and PERHAPS YOUR PROPHETIC OFFICE. At all times, however you must respect others around you who may or may not be open to what you have to share.

Chapter Two Assignment:

PROPHESY TO AN "UNKNOWN RECIPIENT
After studying the material in this chapter your assignment is to

prophesy to a person whose name is not revealed to you. Don't worry about who it is for this will be explained in the next chapter. Don't look ahead or you will spoil the learning opportunity.

There are many levels of information available to you when you prophesy to someone. You will get cues from their appearance, demeanor, emotional state, etc. What you need to realize is that it is ok to feel after what God is saying by making note of information you gather from the individual you are prophesying over. However there are times that you will know absolutely nothing about the person at all. You can still prophesy accurately which this assignment is intended to show.

When you prophesy to someone, in addition to asking permission you should always ask for feedback at an appropriate time. Was the prophecy accurate in any way that they can tell? Was it encouraging? These two factors vastly determine the quality of the word in the target recipient's life. Even if the person is vague or even negative in their feedback just take it as a learning opportunity and keep working at it, keep practicing. Fluency in your prophetic gift will come over time.

Now record on audio or write down a prophetic word to someone that you have no idea who it is. How do you do this? You pray in tongues for at least a minute or two and then go quiet. In the quietness listen for the first word, picture, sound, image whatever comes to you. It doesn't have to be profound or sound spiritual. If you aren't sure what it means ask the Father to reveal this. If nothing else just say what you see, hear or feel. In other words you begin by typing or recording, "I see a _____", or "I sense this _____."
Expect having begun that additional information will come. If it does not that's ok just fall back to a prophetic pray as we taught in chapter one. Start praying for the person (recording or typing) and pray out your heart toward them. When you are finished set the recording aside or save what you have typed and continue to the next chapter.

CHAPTER THREE: RECEIVING A GROUP WORD

INTRODUCTION:

Note: in the last chapter we asked you to prophesy to an "unknown recipient." We will reveal who that is in the assignment section of this chapter.

The time will come in your life that flowing in the prophetic will come with ease and fluency. To help you till then we use these structured activations to give you something to start with as you attempt and in fact do hear from the Father in your heart.

The step-by-step process of activation we use each week is intended to be something you are familiar and comfortable with. As you read each chapter we will introduce new variations and challenges to help you identify how the gifts of the Spirit flow uniquely in you and through you.

Remember that you don't have to hurry. Don't allow yourself to get tensed up and try too hard. The Spirit of God will draw back if you are straining and pushing yourself to produce. Relax. Close your eyes and look within. The scriptures tell us in Col. 1:27 that "Christ in You is the Hope of Glory." The gifts of the Spirit don't fall on you like some foreign influence. They are an inward resource as familiar and comfortable as the indwelling of Jesus on the throne of your heart.

Find that place where Jesus dwells in your heart and put your attention and focus on Him. Notice how your "spiritual eyes" function through your own imagination and your native thoughts. Notice how your "spiritual hearing" manifests the voice of God WITHIN, in the acoustics of your own inner man. The voice of God is much more an inward echo than an outward manifestation.

Pay attention as you "sense to feel" after what God would have you share with the a target group in this activation. It doesn't have to be fully formed at all. Just give your best sense and allow the words and expressions to flow from the Spirit of Christ inside you and out to the group through your sharing.

It is really important not to rush into this and be over and done with it. Allow the Father to call you as *"Deep calleth to Deep"*. Realize that the Holy Spirit wants you to allow Him to take you deep into Himself to build that sensitivity and recognition of His Voice inside you. This is the primary purpose of this course, to hear His voice and share it with others in a positive and convincing way.

THIS WEEK'S ACTIVATION INCLUDES RECEIVING A WORD FOR A GROUP:

You must begin to see yourself as someone God wants to speak through. In our religious culture there are strong misconceptions about where the responsibilities of ministry lie. Consider the following verse with new eyes:

> *(Ephesians 4:11-12) - 11 And he gave some, apostles; and some, prophets; and some, evangelists; and some, pastors and teachers; 12 For the perfecting of the saints for the work of the ministry for the edifying of the body of Christ:*

Traditionally we read the above verse and conclude that the "Five-fold Minister" (i.e. Apostle, Prophet, Evangelist, Pastor, or Teacher) is responsible for the work of the ministry and the edification of the body. That is not what this passage actually says. It actually reads that the "Five-fold Minister" is responsible "for the perfecting (equipping and maturing) of the saints FOR the work of the ministry, for the edifying of the body of Christ."

In short, it isn't the pastor's exclusive job to minister, it is the pastor's job to train and equip YOU for ministry. What is that ministry? To edify the body of Christ. According to the scripture, what is the specific way that you are equipped to edify the body?

> *(1 Corinthians 14:3) - 3 But he that prophesieth speaketh unto men [to] edification, and exhortation, and comfort.*

The pastor's job is to WORK HIMSELF OUT OF A JOB creating a safe and productive environment for the gift of prophecy and the other gifts to operate. Unfortunately because we have a professional clergy and a competitive spirit between churches, many pastors are far too near-sighted and insecure to fulfill this central mandate of the gospel. Instead they create an environment of lethargy, dependence and entitlement among believers that stifles growth and hinders the development of the body and individual believers in their callings and gifting from God.

The Father never intended for a select professional clergy to carry the whole responsibility of ministering to the needs of the people. No one man can possibly meet the needs of all who come for ministry, therefore leaders are to equip all of us, (the saints) to do the work of the ministry, caring for each other, looking out for each other and loving one another in the context of relationship and fellowship.

The saints (including YOU) are the ones called to lay hands on the sick and see them healed, to raise the dead, to heal the blind eyes, to see the broken made whole, and to reach a lost and desperately hurting world come to know the person of Jesus Christ.

LEARNING TO FLOW PROPHETICALLY BEFORE A GROUP OF PEOPLE LARGE OR SMALL

In this chapter's activation, you will also be given an opportunity to receive a Word of Knowledge for a group as a whole. This is known as a CORPORATE WORD as compared to a PERSONAL WORD. In preparation for this choose a church, a small group or even a family you know and love to prophesy over as a unit. If you are studying this material in a classroom or small group setting then that is your target group.

This activation facilitates your ability to share prophetically with a group in addition to individuals. You will be seeking to bring a word that will connect with the whole group.

What you share may involve another gift of the Spirit called a word of knowledge:

In other words, you may "hear" that someone in the group has a pain or discomfort in their body and that God wants to minister healing. In addition to speaking exhortation over a group this type of gift might operate as well. When you single out an individual in the context of ministering to a group, this is known as a "call out".

You may receive a word of knowledge for someone in the group and not know whom the word is for. Go ahead and share what you have. You may find upon getting the results that the intended recipient will know and identify themselves to the rest of the group. Don't place limits on how the Holy Spirit will use you. Simply "look to see," "sense to feel," and "listen to hear". Then share what you have.

This activation will come quite easily if you just relax and rest, trusting that God is faithful and that He wants to speak to you more than you want to hear.

STEP BY STEP PROCESS OF THIS ACTIVATION:

Understand That We Will Share from the Resource of Christ IN Us.

(Colossians 1:27) - 27 To whom God would make known what [is] the riches of the glory of this mystery among the Gentiles; which is Christ in you, the hope of glory:

Christ in you is the key to moving in the gifts. These gifts are not foreign, outward "somethings" that come down like "pennies from heaven." These gifts, what you are to share will distil within you, through your "knower." You will see, hear, feel, or sense something and it will be up to you to trust God to allow you to share accurately and boldly.

We all have Christ living within us. Allow him to minister to you and through you.

1 Peter 4:10 Each one should use whatever gift he has received to serve others, faithfully administering God's grace in its various forms.

Notice the verse above doesn't leave anyone out. EVERY ONE of us has a level of giftedness that represents our responsibility for service in the Kingdom of God. Don't you want to be good stewards of God's grace? Be willing to share Christ within you with the group in this activation.

STIR YOURSELF UP SPIRITUALLY.

How do we stir ourselves up? First, be convinced that it is the Lord's will for every believer to move in the Gifts of the Spirit. Be persuaded that the gifts of the Spirit are present and available because Jesus lives inside of you and He is the one that ministers the gifts. He is the one that qualifies you and chooses you to be a blessing to others.

This is a safe learning environment. Realize that no believer is perfect and it is OK to make a mistake. We all learn by doing. Praying in the Spirit activates the Mind of Christ on the inside of you so that your human spirit can pass on to others the thoughts, impressions, pictures, etc. from the Holy Spirit.

PRAYER OF ACTIVATION:

Pray this prayer before you begin:

> *Father, I come into your presence knowing that you accept me and love me not because of who I am but because of who Jesus is and what he did for me 2000 years ago on the cross. You live in Me. Your presence inside of Me makes Me clean and qualifies Me to serve and be a blessing to others and to this group. You love each of them as much as you love me. I yield every thought to the Spirit of Christ inside of me.*
>
> *I open myself to the Holy Spirit to receive your thoughts, impressions, and leadings for this group or for any particular individual in this group. I will joyfully share just what you show me, and trust that it will be all of you and none of me. I will not doubt or question I will just give what now comes to me. I am a believer, and I expect to receive. I thank you, Father for giving me words of prophecy, and words of knowledge and wisdom from your throne. Amen.*

This prayer given above releases your guilt, fear, condemnation or any sense of unworthiness. Fear and feeling unworthy are the two greatest hindrances to moving in the Gifts of the Spirit. Be bold to believe you CAN share and ARE qualified by Jesus to share His love with others and with your target group in particular.

PRAYER AND PROTECTION:

The short prayer above is also intended to stifle any distraction or religious attitudes and to release your faith and stir up the anointing on the inside of you. Feel free to use whatever words you choose for this but it does not have to be long and involved.

Now, go silent in order to listen, look and feel. Relax! This is supposed to be fun. Just get still and allow yourself to tune in to the Holy Spirit. After you go silent give yourself about a minute to look and see what might form in your mind's eye. Listen to hear in your Spirit and also focus on any sense of what you feel in your knower the Spirit of God might be leading you to share.

REVIEWING THE DIFFERENT WAYS GOD MAY SPEAK TO YOU:

Again, here is an explanation different modes of receiving prophetically from God on the inside of you:

If you are one who "sees", you will see pictures in your mind quite easily. These images may involve interpretation but don't get stuck on that. Just give exactly what you see in your mind. We will help you with interpretations later.

If you are one who is a "hearer," then on the inside of you will come an acoustic impression of what the Spirit of God is saying. This won't often be in an audible voice but for some of you it could be. Usually, however you just feel like you are hearing something. In the natural you are not hearing anything audible but you still feel as if you are hearing what you receive. Once you hear, you simply share what you hear the Spirit saying to you.

If you are one who "feels" or "senses," you simply sense and know something that it feels right but you could not explain to anyone how this came to you. You "just know"! That is ok. The "sensing to feel" modality is the subtlest of the different ways to hear from God. Sometimes, particularly with regard to healing and discerning pain you may actually feel something for someone else. For instance, God may give you a word of knowledge of a physical healing He wants to do by allowing you to briefly feel the condition that God desires to heal in your own body. This is called a "physical word of knowledge".

Chapter Three Assignment:

NOW, GIVE YOUR WORD ACCORDING TO THE SPIRIT'S LEADING.

This is the doing part for which we have prepared ourselves. Prepare you notepad, recording device, or to type what you receive from the Father. Specifically describe EXACTLY what the Holy Spirit showed you, being cautious not to add any of your own interpretation. After you get this word from the Father feel free to keep it private for "practice" only or if you wish share it with the group and ask for feedback.

We also want to re-state our caution mentioned previously which is: God does not give us judgmental, negative, harsh, corrective, or directive words. For the scope of these exercises, these types of words will be STRICTLY OFF LIMITS. If you believe you receive one of these types of words during the activation exercise, assume you have heard wrong and go back to the Lord and ask Him for a different thought from God for your group.

Remember, you will be looking for a simple "word" of prophecy that will connect with the whole group or an individual within the group. After you forward on what you get, it will be shared with what the other interns give next week.

WHO WAS THE UNKNOWN RECIPIENT:

The unknown recipient in the last chapter you prophesied over was YOU. By choosing this little obfuscation we have given you the thrill and privilege to prophesy to yourself! Now go back over the word and regard it as though it came from someone else: Is it accurate? Is it encouraging? If so, GREAT! If it is not accurate don't be disappointed. Practice makes perfect. Fluency comes with consistent effort. You won't start out with powerful, awesome words with supernatural accuracy. Just keep moving forward and doing the exercises and you will be blessed by how the Father uses you as you come with humility to make yourself available to bless others.

CHAPTER FOUR: PROPHESYING TO A RANGE OF PEOPLE

ACTIVATING THE SPIRIT OF GOD INSIDE YOU:

Interning in the prophetic involves learning by doing. Therefore we are moving strongly into activations. Some interns find this daunting but bear in mind that the Kingdom of God doesn't come by observation (Luke 17:20). The gifts of the Spirit are activated by cultivation and experimentation. This is why we provide a learning environment where the most important thing you can do is make your best effort. You will find fluency, accuracy and anointing will increase over time.

By now you should have a basic understanding of what activation entails and with this chapter our step-by-step process should start becoming somewhat familiar to you.

I want you to notice that with each chapter, we will be introducing new variations and challenges that are designed to help you continue to stretch and exercise your prophetic gifts. By now it is our hope that you are beginning to grasp the concept of using the using your spiritual "eyes" (visionary response), your "ears" (acoustic response), and your "knower" (perceptive response).

DON'T RUSH THINGS:

We would encourage you not to not rush the activation assignment portion of each chapter but rather allow the Lord to take you as deep as He would choose to build that sensitivity and recognition of His voice in your heart. Hearing the Father's voice is the primary purpose of this course. You don't want to hurry through the activations. Take your time and linger over the activation exercises and use your intuition and the sense of God's spirit inside you to deepen your prophetic gifting.

Having pointed out these things we move on now to the activation assignment for chapter four.

PROPHESYING TO A RANGE OF INDIVIDUALS:

As we touched on in the previous lesson the responsibility of caring for one another and propagating the kingdom is not the sole purview of the clergy (the pastor or "5-fold minister"). Actually the job of the 5-fold ministry (or church leaders) mentioned in Ephesians chapter four is not merely to DO the work of the ministry but to TRAIN THE SAINTS to DO THE WORK OF THE MINISTRY. The job of the clergy is to WORK THEMSELVES OUT OF A JOB. They do this by equipping the believers under their care with the training, gifting and fluency in spiritual gifts that qualifies them to care for themselves and for one another.

MINISTRY IS THE RESPONSBILITY OF ALL BELIEVERS:

> *Eph. 4: 11 And He gave some, apostles; and some, prophets; and some, evangelists; and some, pastors and teachers; 12 For the perfecting of the saints, for the work of the ministry, for the edifying of the body of Christ.*

To Give an Example:

> *1 John 2:27 - But the anointing which ye have received of him abideth in you, and ye need not that any man teach you: but as the same anointing teacheth you of all*

> *things, and is truth, and is no lie, and even as it hath taught you, ye shall abide in him.*

The above verse speaks of the gift of teaching which is one of the 5-fold ministry gifts mentioned in Ephesians chapter four. When the teacher has done his job in your life, he or she has activated the Holy Spirit on the inside of you to teach you to feed yourself and others such as your family the word of God. The anointing IN YOU is CHRIST IN YOU. *Christ in you* is the central theme of the gospel that Paul preached:

> *Col. 1:27 - To whom God would make known what [is] the riches of the glory of this mystery among the Gentiles; which is Christ in you, the hope of glory:*

The anointing in you is the same as Christ in you. The gifts of the Spirit, including prophecy proceed from the indwelling of God's spirit on the inside of you. The 5-fold ministry is given to the earth not simply to BE these things TO you, but rather to ACTIVATE THESE ANOINTINGS ON THE INSIDE OF YOU.

The teacher is a teacher anointed of God yes this is true. But his purpose is not merely to teach you but also to further equip you to feed yourself and others on the good word of God. The prophet, when he does his job, not only prophesies to you, but he ACTIVATES the voice of God on the inside of you. This is the very heart of my calling and that of my spouse: To bring you the voice of the Father and activate the voice of the Father in you so you can hear him for yourself.

In this chapter you will be given a range of names and will be asked to minister to one, two or the whole number of them individually. You will draw these names out of the group you are studying with or from your family, small group or church group.

PURPOSE OF STANDING BEFORE A GROUP OF PEOPLE IN PROPHECY:

This type of ministry is sometimes called a "call out" as we have mentioned before. This type of prophetic ministry involves you considering each person in this group and replying back what the Father may be saying to you for one, two or each of them in turn. This may include a word of knowledge for healing of the body as well:

You may look at a name on your list and get a sense or even a physical feeling in your body that is actually a word of knowledge for healing of the person you are considering. Don't hesitate to speak this out. In fact over each person you prophesy to the less you think about it and simply act to speak out the more accurate you will be.

You may look at one of the names in the list in this activation and receive a word of knowledge for someone else in their life, such as a daughter, son or spouse. Don't hesitate to give what you have.

You may also look at the group and get a word but not know exactly whom the word is for. Go ahead and give that as well and if that person is in the group we trust they will speak up.

We do not want to place limits on what the Holy Spirit may say but rather encourage you to simply listen to whatever He says and then be faithful to speak this to the individual or group.

Receiving a Word of Knowledge is one of the most exciting and rewarding gifts to operate in through the prophetic. It is exciting for you to know that God is indeed speaking through you and exciting to the person you speak over to know that God cares enough to single them out.

STEP BY STEP PROCESS OF THIS ACTIVATION:

This process remains essentially the same as the activations we presented you with in the previous weeks. Bear in mind you are sharing from the "Christ in you". This isn't being "psychic" or "clairvoyant". There is a huge difference between moving in the gifts of God and manifesting a spirit of divination. Divination is about controlling and manipulating people. The gifts of the Spirit of God are about liberating and freeing people.

Focus on the fact that you have Christ living within you. As you look at the names below allow Him to minister through you and to your brother or sister in Christ.

In preparation, stir yourself up spiritually. How do we do that?

First, be convinced that it is the Lord's will for every believer to move in the gifts of the Spirit. Next, be persuaded that you have all the gifts of God in you by the indwelling of Christ. When Jesus ascended he gave gifts to men (and women). You have the gifting of God on the inside of you. Believe it will activate and be accurate and a blessing to the people you minister to.

Realize that no believer is perfect and it is OK to make a mistake. This is a safe training environment. Just know that we all learn by doing

Praying in the Spirit (in tongues) also acts as a catalyst to receive the mind of Christ so that our human spirit can receive thoughts, impressions, pictures, etc. from the Holy Spirit. We activate the gifts by faith and grace, therefore it is our responsibility.

Pray a Brief Prayer:

Pray this prayer over yourself as you begin:

> *Dear Lord, In the name of Your Son, Jesus Christ, I come before Your throne. I am washed by the blood. Christ lives within me. Not just in part, but in my whole being. I bring every thought of my mind and soul into captivity to the mind of Christ. I will be open to be led by the Holy Spirit to receive a thought or impression from You for this group or for an individual in this group. I will gladly share just what you show me, without adding my own interpretation to it. I will not doubt it nor question it, I'll just be willing to give it. I am a believer, and I expect to receive. I thank You for giving me a word of knowledge from the throne. Amen.*

This prayer releases you from any guilt, fear, condemnation and sense of unworthiness. Since fear and feeling unworthy are the two things that hinder people most, this prayer brings a release so you can let yourself be used of God.

Now: be silent and listen, look and feel. Take a look at the names in your group and one by one see what the Father begins to share with you for them. Move through the names without hesitation.

Now relax and "tune in" to the Holy Spirit. Once you go silent, give yourself a moment and during this pause, look and see what pictures form in your mind's eye (the eyes of your heart), listen to what you may hear in your Spirit and pay attention to what sense you may have in your "knower".

Again, here is an explanation of these different modes of receiving:

If you are a "seer", you will see pictures in your mind readily. These pictures may require interpretation but you are to give exactly what you see in your mind for now. We will deal with interpretations later.

If you are a "hearer", you will "hear" what the Spirit says. This will not usually be an audible voice but for some of you it could be - on rare occasion. Normally, you just feel like you are hearing something. In actuality, you are not hearing anything audible but you still feel as if you are hearing what you receive. Once you hear, you simply share what you hear the Spirit saying to you for your target recipients one by one.

If you are a "knower / feeler", you just seem to know something and it feels right but you could not explain to anyone how you know, you just know! It is like a built in sense of "what is". If you are a knower, you will recognize this pattern. If you are a feeler, you may actually feel something. For instance, God may give you a word of knowledge of a physical healing He wants to do by allowing you to briefly feel the condition that God desires to heal in your own body. This is called a "physical word of knowledge.

Chapter Four Assignment:

TIME TO ACT, YOU LEARN BY DOING:

Now, go back and look at the names and record your word for them according to the Spirit's leading. Then proceed to the internship forum provided (see your welcome e-mail or the weekly e-mail for access link).

This is the doing part for which we have prepared ourselves. Use your computer, a notepad, smart phone or recording device to pecifically describe EXACTLY what the Holy Spirit showed you, being cautious not to add any of your own interpretation.

We also want to re-state our caution which is: "God does not give us judgmental, negative, harsh, corrective, or directive words". For the scope of these exercises, these types of words will be STRICTLY OFF LIMITS. If you believe you receive one of these types of words during the activation exercise, assume you have heard wrong and go back to the Lord and ask Him for a different thought from God for your group.

Remember, you will be looking for a simple word of prophecy that will connect with each individual within the group or perhaps each one in your target group. Try not to leave anyone out.

Application:

Imagine yourself on a prayer team or ministry team. How would you use this technique in ministering to individuals in a group of people who come up for prayer? Imagine yourself standing in the midst of a group of those waiting to be prayed for when someone on the ministry team calls out your specific situation by Word of Knowledge and then asks you to some forward for prayer. Would your faith be increased to believe that the Lord had you personally in His mind at that point in time? Absolutely! Since your faith would be boosted as a result, your faith mixed with the faith of the one ministering to you would likely result in you receiving what God had for you at that moment.

CHAPTER FIVE: THE VISIONARY RESPONSE

Introduction:

Beginning in this chapter we will study the core practics of hearing from God: These are the visionary response, the acoustic response and the perceptive response. Obviously there are many ways of communicating with the Father but for the sake of this material we will cover the three primary modalities by which God speaks.

The focus in this chapter will include the SEER MODALITY or the VISIONARY RESPONSE.

The Visionary Response (the Eyes of God):

Receiving a "Word Picture" Activation

The purpose of the activation in this lesson is to learn how to prophesy from pictures that the Father gives you in your heart and mind. It is one thing to receive a picture, after you SEE you must then attempt to describe pictorially what you see and apply it to the target recipient of the word given.

Who Will You Be Prophesying To?

This activation will use a variable "target", which means you get to choose. You can prophesy to a group of your choosing, to any individual in the group; or you can give a word to any other person you feel prompted to minister to. This is up to you. Make the effort to sense to whom the Father wants you to minister and what you should say or do.

Receiving a "Visionary Word":

There is a much mystique surrounding the visionary word or "word picture". What are we talking about essentially? When Peter stood up on the day of Pentecost to explain the strange event of 120 people speaking publicly in other tongues, he didn't quote any verse about tongues themselves. He did however speak of dreams and visions. Have you ever wondered about this?

> *Act 2:14 - 17; verse 14 - But Peter, standing up with the eleven, lifted up his voice, and said unto them, Ye men of Judaea, and all [ye] that dwell at Jerusalem, be this known unto you, and hearken to my words: 15 - For these are not drunken, as ye suppose, seeing it is [but] the third hour of the day. 16 - But this is that which was spoken by the prophet Joel; 17 - And it shall come to pass in the last days, saith God, I will pour out of my Spirit upon all flesh: and your sons and your daughters shall prophesy, and your young men shall see visions, and your old men shall dream dreams:*

There are several Old Testament verses that point to speaking in other tongues. Peter could have used any one of these verses to point at the 120 and said *"this is what they are doing and why they are doing it"*. One of the verses he could have quoted was:

> *Isa 28:11 KJV - For with stammering lips and another tongue will he speak to this people.*

Nonetheless, Peter DID NOT quote ANY verses that spoke about the gift of tongues! Rather he quoted a verse from Joel that declared that in the last days there would be a people (us included) whose lives were earmarked by DREAMS and VISIONS. We will cover dreams in future material but today we are going to encourage you to open yourself to the visionary response of the Holy Spirit.

> *Joel 2:28 KJV - And it shall come to pass afterward, [that] I will pour out my spirit upon all flesh; and your sons and your daughters shall prophesy, your old men shall dream dreams, your young men shall see visions:*

Now I ask you, which is more acceptable in the average church that claims to accept "Charismatic or Pentecostal" truth? Is it more acceptable to pray in tongues, or to stand up during a testimony time and say *"I want to share a dream or a vision"?* In most of the more traditional groups it is more or less acceptable to give a message in tongues or to pray in tongues. However dreams, visions or claiming that God is speaking directly to you is many times frowned upon as unsafe or untrustworthy. Such giftings are relegated to the prayer room or the after-glow service where they can be contained, controlled and minimalized.

From the biblical standpoint DREAMS and VISIONS are not JUST for someone in the office of a prophet! Peter quoted and Joel proclaimed that EVERYONE, "all flesh" would have dreams and visions not just the super spiritual or the elite prophetic ministry. So in this material don't start with the assumption that God WILL NOT speak to you in dreams or visions. God WANTS to speak to you, He probably IS speaking all the time through the visionary response, you simply need to open yourself to Him. This material will help you in this regard.

What If We Are Deceived?

I get this question a lot. Interns don't want to miss God. They don't want to give a vision in error or a false vision that supposedly came from the devil. Let me assure you, this doesn't happen as often as you might think. Most people believe they are more prone to NOT hear from God than they are to hear His voice. Consider the next verse:

> *John 10:3 - To him the porter openeth; and the sheep hear his voice: and he calleth his own sheep by name, and leadeth them out. 4 - And when he putteth forth his own sheep, he goeth before them, and the sheep follow him: for they know his voice. 5 - And a stranger will they not follow, but will flee from him: for they know not the voice of strangers.*

Ask yourself, *"how do I assure that what I hear is God's voice and not my own or the devil's?."* Read the scripture above. *"... a stranger they will not follow."* Who won't follow the wrong voice? The answer is *"the sheep"* won't follow the wrong voice. Are you one of God's sheep? Then as long as you LIVE OUT OF YOUR "SHEEP NATURE" BEFORE THE LORD you will not be deceived. So let that comfort you, as a sheep of the shepherd that He will help you know you are hearing from Him as you yield and share what you have received.

The first part of receiving from God through the visionary response is the act of getting pictures of revelation. Now where do these pictures come from? You need to know that visions are spiritual in nature and originate from God. However in communicating them to you, at some point they have to be presented by God Himself through the palette or instrumentality of your own human nature, in this case your *IMAGINATION*.

Your imagination is that part of yourself that God created to receive and store pictures and images, whether they are still pictures or pictures in sequence such as a video or movie.

The important thing is WHAT CHANNEL are you tuning your imagination to? Are you tuning to the worry channel? Or some other inappropriate channel? Now at this point in our class someone usually says, *"I don't understand, I don't see anything."* OK, let me help you. I will turn on your internal television. Are you ready?

Demystifying the Prophetic: Prophetic Activation Internship

Don't think of a pink elephant.

Now you saw a pink elephant when I said that. Without any cooperation from you, I tuned you in to the Russ Walden channel of Silliness. God will activate you in the same way but it won't be silly it will be something intended to help someone. You have always said you want to be used of God and this is the simplicity of getting started.

For this exercise and activation we are tuning to the GOD CHANNEL (the one with broadcast facilities in heaven, not the one in the United Kingdom – no offense to God.tv).

Now to prepare yourself for this activation we want you to know the value of going silent and listening as best you can for a few moments before sharing with someone. This clears your mind of all human and mental clutter so that you can receive what the Father will cause to bubble up in your spirit by the Holy Spirit.

Once something comes to you, for the purpose of this activation, write it down somewhere. It doesn't matter what it is. Just write down the first picture you get. Now how do you prophesy that picture? Go look at the list of names in your group or the list you came up with yourself if you are studying this material independently. If one of the names stands out to you, then choose that name as the focus of your prophetic picture prophecy.

Next, break the picture down into its different elements. For example tree, sun, water, bird, etc. Bearing in mind the focus or chosen "target" of your sharing, (individual or group) as you come to the different elements of the picture, you then take the element and prophesy it into the person or group.

Feel free to use descriptive poetic adjectives to describe each element of the picture. For example is you see the sun how to do you prophesy that into someone?

> *For surely the Lord says son or daughter the light of My glory is getting ready to shine upon you. You will feel the warmth of My presence as I shine My light of revelation upon you.*

Do you see how this works? You take what you see, hear or feel and prophesy that into the person as edification, exhortation and comfort.

Remember the Purpose:
I know this will challenge many of you. This material is about stretching yourself and doing things that may be uncomfortable to you. Do you want to activate the prophetic? Remember this is a learning environment, you can't make a mistake. The biggest mistake is to not participate at all.

The purpose of this activation is to learn how to prophesy picture revelations and to learning descriptive language to paint what you see, and then how to personalize spiritually the elements of the picture you see and prophesy it into the target person or group.

Ready? Go through a Step by Step Process of this Activation:
Now just take yourself through the steps (consulting the target list you have been assigned to or one you came up with independently).

Understand That We Will Share from the Christ Within Us
Since we are all saved, we have Christ living within us. Let's allow Him to minister

to us, through us, and to and through our brother or sister in Christ. The testimony of Jesus is the Spirit of Prophecy so you are simply allowing who Jesus is on the inside of you to stand up and speak His love and truth to the person you are praying over.

> *1 Peter 4:10 Each one should use whatever gift he has received to serve others, faithfully administering God's*

grace in its various forms.

We want to be good stewards of God's grace so let's be willing to share Christ within us with our brother or sister.

Stir Yourself Up Spiritually: How Do We Stir Ourselves Up?

First, be convinced that it is the Lord's will for every believer to move in the Gifts of the Spirit. Next, be persuaded that you have at least 1 of the 9 gifts. Pray in tongues for at least a minute or to right now. If you don't pray in tongues we can help you with that, just contact us.

Eph. 4:7-8 tells us: *But to EACH ONE OF US* (including you) *grace has been given as Christ apportioned it.*

This is why it says: *"When he ascended on high, he led captives in his train and gave gifts to men."* Realize that no believer is perfect and it is OK to make a mistake. If you believe these verses you must acknowledge that the gift of God and the gift of prophecy is in you. As you apply yourself and make the effort in time fluency will come and greater anointing and impact to bless along with it for those you share with.

Just Know That We All Learn by Doing

Praying in the Spirit acts as a catalyst to receive the mind of Christ so that our human spirit can receive thoughts, impressions, pictures, etc. from the Holy Spirit

We activate the gifts by faith and grace, therefore it is our responsibility to stir ourselves up.

Activation Prayer

Pray this prayer as you begin:

> *Dear Lord, In the name of Your Son, Jesus Christ, I come before Your throne. I am washed by the blood. Christ lives within me. Not just in part, but in my whole being. I bring every thought of my mind and soul into captivity*

> to the mind of Christ. I will be open to be led by the Holy Spirit to receive a thought or impression from You for this group or for the corporate church. I will gladly share just what you show me, without adding my own interpretation to it. I will not doubt it nor question it, I'll just be willing to give it. I am a believer, and I expect to receive. I thank You for giving me a word of knowledge from the throne. Amen.

This prayer releases people from fear, condemnation or any sense of unworthiness. Since fear and feeling unworthy are the two most hindering factors to people moving in the mind of Christ, this prayer is intended to bring a release from these hindrances.

Also pray a brief prayer of protection over yourself. The purpose of this short and specific prayer is also to bind any hindering or religious spirits and to release faith and anointing. Feel free to improvise and use whatever words you choose for this but it does not have to be long and involved.

Now, Be Silent And Listen, Look And Feel
Relax because this is going to be fun as you tune in to the Holy Spirit. Once you go silent, give yourself about 45 - 60 seconds to look and see what pictures form in your minds eye (the eyes of your heart.

Again, Here is an Explanation of the Primary Modalities by Which God Speaks:
If you are more gifted as a "seer", you will see pictures in your mind readily. These pictures may require interpretation but you are to give exactly what you see in your mind for now. If the visionary response is not the primary way you hear from God, nonetheless you can still receive pictures, impressions, and mental images to share in this activation so you will be familiar with how this modality works.

Now, Give Your Word For Your Chosen Target (Either Individual or the Group According To The Spirit's Leading)

This is the doing part we for which we have prepared ourselves. Now is the time to, one person at a time, speak specifically what the Holy Spirit showed you. Again, we re-state our caution from the activation from previous weeks:

> *God does not usually give us judgmental, negative, harsh, corrective, or directive words when we are just learning to move in the prophetic. For the scope of these exercises, these types of words will be STRICTLY OFF LIMITS. If you believe you receive one of these types of words during the activation exercise, assume you have heard wrong and go back to the Lord and ask Him for a different thought from God for your group.*

From our original purpose paragraph, you will be looking for a picture or impression that you will then describe as best you can what you think the Spirit is saying. Remember fluency comes with practice. If you don't get much just share what you have.

Application

Imagine yourself in a worship portion of a meeting in your local church. You feel you hear the Lord quickening something in your spirit for the church body as a whole. You suddenly and strongly SEE a picture in your heart or mind. Will you have the faith to believe that you can in fact SEE accurately enough to be willing to share what you hear with the congregation? Will fear become a deterrent to your being willing to be a vessel for delivering a corporate word?

As you review the scripture in 1 Cor. 14:26:

> *"What then shall we say, brothers? When you come together, everyone has a hymn, or a word of instruction, a revelation, a tongue or an interpretation. All of these must be done for the strengthening of the church."*

Do you see yourself fitting into this pattern as the scripture directs? How much more alive in the Spirit would our meetings and gatherings be if instead of coming together to get spiritually what we can from others, we all came together to share what the Lord had already given us for the benefit (overall strengthening) of the Body?

One word of caution on giving corporate words - if any of us are still harboring wounds that need to draw attention to themselves, the enemy will try to work through your wounding to use this type of setting to draw attention to us instead of pointing toward the Lord and giving Him glory. The safeguard to this is to always be willing to submit anything you receive for the corporate body to the church leadership and allow them to make the determination as to how the word fits into the flow of the service. Resist using the prophetic to direct the flow of the service or groups in the church unless the church leadership gives you release to publicly speak.

Go ahead now give your visionary prophetic words over each recipient chosen by you or assigned to you by a group leader. Even if you don't have anything just start out. Don't be timid you can't make a mistake.

CHAPTER SIX: THE ACOUSTIC RESPONSE

Receiving From God Through The Acoustic (Or Audible) Response

Developing Ears To Hear

Each of the five senses has a spiritual counterpart. Prophet Kitty teaches in her prophetic training courses that we "look to see, listen to hear, sense to feel" what the Father is saying to us. In the last chapter we taught on the VISIONARY RESPONSE which involves seeing what God is saying. The acoustic response is about HEARING what God is saying. Again, here are the primary modalities by which the Father commonly speaks:

THE VISIONARY RESPONSE:
Seeing what God is Saying

THE ACOUSTIC RESPONSE:
Hearing what God is Saying

THE PERCEPTIVE RESPONSE:
Feeling what God is Saying

Jesus said no less than eight times "he that has ears to hear let him hear..." It might do some good to review those verses here:

Matthew 11:15 He that hath ears to hear, let him hear.

Matthew 13:9, 43 Who hath ears to hear, let him hear. ... (43) Then shall the righteous shine forth as the sun in the kingdom of their Father. Who hath ears to hear, let him hear.

Mark 4:9, 23 And he said unto them, He that hath ears to hear, let him hear. ... (23) If any man have ears to hear, let him hear.

Mark 7:16 If any man have ears to hear, let him hear.

Luke 8:8 And other fell on good ground, and sprang up, and bare fruit an hundredfold. And when he had said these things, he cried, He that hath ears to hear, let him hear.

Luke 14:35 It is neither fit for the land, nor yet for the dunghill; [but] men cast it out. He that hath ears to hear, let him hear.

These references total eight in number and it is interesting to note that the number eight in scripture is the number, which denotes "new beginnings." Hearing the voice of the Father is the preamble to the next thing God is going to do in your life. He will not do anything in your life without first speaking to you in regard to His plans. We hear from God for others if we are prophetic but we also must learn to hear from God for ourselves.

Jesus received the words of the Father through the visionary response:

John 5:19 Then answered Jesus and said unto them, Verily, verily, I say unto you, The Son can do nothing of himself, but what he seeth the Father do: for what things soever he doeth, these also doeth the Son likewise.

Demystifying the Prophetic: Prophetic Activation Internship

Jesus also received directions from the Father through the acoustic response or "hearing the voice of the Father":

> John 5:30 I can of mine own self do nothing: as I hear, I judge: and my judgment is just; because I seek not mine own will, but the will of the Father which hath sent me.

There are many different ways to hear what God is saying. They can range anywhere from the fully audible voice of God all the way to the other side of the scale, involving the faintest impression of God's inward voice in your heart.

The intensity of the voice does not determine the validity of what you hear. One of the problems with the acoustic response is sorting out the other voices you might hear.

> 1 Corinthians 14:10 There are, it may be, so many kinds of voices in the world, and none of them [is] without signification.

How do you know what you are hearing (whether it is outwardly audible or just an inward impression) how do you know that you are hearing from God?

The standard response to this question is usually "does what you hear line up with the word of God?"

It is true, if the voice that comes to you blatantly contradicts scripture then you know you aren't hearing the valid voice of the Father. Or is it? Now in this course I ask you, do you want to be treated like children, or do you want to be taught as though you were bona fide, mature men and women of God?

Then consider the following:

God will never contradict His word when He speaks to you. However He will

OFTEN speak to you contrary to YOUR UNDERSTANDING of the word of

God.

In other words, you may look at a person and make certain conclusions about them that you think line up with the word of God. But then to your dismay the Father tells you something about that person that contradicts your perception and your understanding of the word. Does it mean you heard wrong? No, God will never contradict His word, but He often knows more about people and situations than we do. Prepare yourself for the fact that He will speak through you according to His infinite knowledge and you must be diligent to speak what He gives you.

Again this is not to suggest that the Father contradicts His written word. The written word is the LOGOS of God. The prophetic word is the RHEMA (utterance) of God.

There is a delicate balance between the LOGOS (established, written word of God) and the RHEMA (uttered) word of God. This is because the RHEMA is very often the contemporary clarification and application of the LOGOS that is needed to bring us the full value of what God is saying.

Modalities Of Hearing The Father:

The Audible Voice:
Part of your assignment in this chapter is to record in writing an anecdote about some experience you have recently had with HEARING the voice of God. Many people think about hearing God and they might remember a television commercial for a drain-cleaning product. In the commercial a disembodied voice booms out to the customer "WOULD DRAINO LET YOU HURT YOUR PIPES?" That may be comical to think about, but that is seldom how God speaks, even in the recorded instances that bible figures heard His voice.

When Jesus raised Lazarus God spoke over Him in such a way that even bystanders could hear it. This is the greatest intensity that God speaks by:

> *John 12:28-29 ... Then came there a voice from heaven, [saying], I have both glorified [it], and will glorify [it] again. (29) The people therefore, that stood by, and heard [it], said that it thundered: others said, An angel spake to him.*

Don't be surprised if in preparation for the activation in this chapter that you hear the voice of the Father in such a way that those around you in your home hear something as well. Although if you notice, even though Jesus understood the voice, those nearby didn't hear it so clearly as to realize what was said or that it was even the voice of God speaking. They confused the voice of God with thunder or some other natural phenomena. God will often speak to you, but you must be astute enough to listen to what is going on around you. What you might discount as some naturally occurring noise in your home or environment might in fact be the voice of God speaking.

This is why Kitty insists that when something out of the ordinary happens (something that makes you do a double take) you must PRAY TO INTERPRET so you are hearing what the voice of God may be saying.

The Still Small Voice:
Hearing the voice of God also comes quietly as a still small voice.

> *1 Kings 19:12 And after the earthquake a fire; [but] the LORD [was] not in the fire: and after the fire a still small voice.*

In the verse above, God was teaching the prophet that He didn't always speak with great fanfare or massive signs. We need to attune ourselves to listen. God is always speaking but we are not always listening.

Another way God speaks is through the voice of someone familiar to us:

> *1 Samuel 3:9 KJV Therefore Eli said unto Samuel, Go, lie down: and it shall be, if he call thee, that thou shalt say, Speak, LORD; for thy servant heareth. So Samuel went and lay down in his*

place.

The child Samuel grew up to be one of the greatest prophets in the Old Testament. When God began speaking to Samuel as a child, He spoke to him in the voice of the father figure in his life. In my own case for 34 years the Father spoke to me in a voice that sounded like my natural father, Roy Walden. That wasn't odd to me because it so happens that my natural father is also my spiritual father and it seemed normal for God to use a voice that sounded like my Dad to speak to me.

Then came the day that the voice changed. I knew it immediately and asked the Father why he had changed how he spoke to me. He answered me and said "I will no longer speak to you in the voice of your natural father, but I will speak to you in my native voice because today you have become a man."

The Voice of God Distils Within Your Heart:
So there are many different modalities for hearing the Father's voice. I want to mention one more. This next way God speaks is the subtlest. Read the following verse:

> *Deuteronomy 32:2 My doctrine shall drop as the rain, my speech shall distil as the dew, as the small rain upon the tender herb, and as the showers upon the grass:*

Notice the word distil. Let's do an experiment that will help you understand how the voice of God will DISTIL in your spirit: Take a glass of ice water and set it in front of you. Notice that at first there doesn't appear to be any condensation on the outside of the glass. Then seemingly without realizing it the glass is dripping with water that has distilled on the outside. The voice of God many times will come to you this way. For me it is the most common way He talks to me. I will be going about my day minding my own business and suddenly the words of God are there in my spirit having distilled there without my realizing it.

Activation Assignment:

This chapter's assignment is to minister over a group of recipients (at least 5) that your group leader may choose or if you are working independently a list of your own. Remember you are practicing so don't allow yourself to become stressed out or overburdened. Learn to minister from a place of rest.

NOTE: Just for fun I would like you in your sharing to see what the Father might tell you something about your recipient that you don't actually know in the natural (where they live; what they do for a living). This is the "word of knowledge" portion of the prophetic and making this effort encourages you to be more fluent in this aspect of the gift.

So you are going to tune in to God and believe for a word for each recipient and then be willing to step out in faith to HEAR what God is saying. In the last chapter we exercised the VISIONARY RESPONSE but this week I want you to make the effort to HEAR in the Spirit what the Father says over each.

Purpose:
This week's activation also includes purposely seeking a word of knowledge for each recipient (where they live, what they do for a living. This will allow you to tune into any area of each recipient's life, from ministry, future ministry, home, personal life, etc.

Not only will we be fulfilling God's desire to communicate, but also we will hear a wide variety of words that can be given to one person. This in turn helps us to gain understanding of the unlimited ways in which God chooses to share.

CHAPTER SEVEN: THE PERCEPTIVE RESPONSE

The Perceptive Response: Sensing to Feel

Receiving From God Through The Perceptive Response Or Sensing To Feel

As mentioned in last chapter, each of the five senses has a spiritual counterpart. Prophet Kitty teaches in her prophetic training courses that we "look to see, listen to hear, sense to feel." In the last chapter we taught on the ACOUSTIC RESPONSE, which involves hearing what God is saying.

To review, here are the primary modalities by which the Father commonly speaks:

> VISIONARY RESPONSE: Seeing what God is Saying
>
> ACOUSTIC RESPONSE: Hearing what God is Saying
>
> PERCEPTIVE RESPONSE: Feeling what God is Saying

When you consider the ways in which God speaks you begin to see that the body, soul and spirit of a person represent a unified palette through which the Father communicates. You are made up of a spirit, soul and body. The Father through the

Holy Spirit uses these three components of your person to speak to you in different ways.

Bodily Experiences: God Communicates Through The Physical Body And The Five Senses

From the perspective of sensing to feel we can legitimately describe the physical body as a complex observation platform into the unseen world of the spirit. Spiritual experiences that impact or arise from the physical body are very profound and moving.

Tactile spiritual experiences, open eye visions and hearing the audible voice of God are not necessarily more valid ways of hearing God but they are certainly visceral and impacting. You have our permission to have as many of these as you like, as long as you share them with the rest of us!

Emotional Experiences: God Communicating Through The Soul

In this chapter we are acquainting you with the PERCEPTIVE response which can and often does manifest in the emotional part of your inner man. You are made up of spirit, soul and body. It is helpful to understand the different components of spirit, soul and body because they are like strings of an instrument the Father will pluck when he speaks to us:

>SPIRIT:
>
>>*(Made up of Intuition, Sentience [self-awareness, God awareness], and Conscience)*
>
>SOUL:
>
>>*(Made up of Mind, Emotions, and Will)*
>
>BODY:

(Made up of Sight, Hearing, Feeling, Tasting, Smelling)

The visionary and acoustic responses taught about in the previous two lessons involve God speaking primarily through the human spirit and also the mind. The perceptive response involves God speaking through the emotions and particularly your physical body. Mystics often experience God at this depth.

Did you ever walk into a room and be inexplicably overwhelmed by a sense of dread or some other strong emotion? Did you ever get that feeling we joke about "someone just walked over my grave?" (We are using negative examples because they are the most common so don't get nervous).

Did you ever make a decision or have a conversation with someone and your tummy was just turning flip-flops on the inside of you? Kitty and I often counsel people "Listen to your tummy. The tummy knows!" This is the perceptive response at work.

The First Witness

The perceptive response or God speaking through your senses is usually the initial way that He speaks in many situations. Have you ever over-ruled your first impression in a situation only to realize later you should have paid attention? This is the perceptive response in action. The perceptive response doesn't need as much cultivating in most people because it is usually quite active already. What needs to be cultivated is a trust in the fact that you are actually hearing!

Out Of Your Belly Shall Flow Rivers Of Living Water

Is there scripture for God speaking in through the perceptive response?

> [Proverbs 20:27 KJV] The spirit of man [is] the candle of the LORD, searching all the inward parts of the belly.

God uses the Holy Spirit in tandem with the physical body to illuminate and communicate to you things He wants you to know. Jesus spoke of God moving through the "belly":

> [John 7:38 KJV] He that believeth on me, as the scripture hath said, out of his belly shall flow rivers of living water.

Your physical body is a point of release for the outpouring of the Holy Spirit in your life. This verse validates what the field of alternative medicine calls the "mind / body connection". However it isn't just the mind involved but the Spirit of God as well.

In reading this you may be having an "ah hah" moment remembering experiences that left you questioning what you felt and what you sensed in situations in the past. The point of teaching on these things is to give you wisdom and confidence to act intelligently the next time the perceptions come to you. You must condition yourself to listen BEFORE the moment passes and the information communicated is no longer as valuable. In other words this should help you listen to God going into a situation not merely figuring it out after the fact.

God's Secret Name That We All Use: "Something Told Me ..."

An example of this is when you are going down the road and SOMETHING inside say "don't take your usual route, go the other way even though it's longer..." Typically then you don't listen and you encounter a delay, an accident or something that makes you realize "I should have listened!"

You may have even had a churning in your belly talking to you stronger and stronger the longer you ignored the guidance. This is not just some human extrasensory experience. It is God's spirit talking to your spirit through your body. It happens all the time even to people who don't consider themselves spiritual or deep feeling at all.

More Scripture On Sensing To Feel:

> [Acts 17:27 KJV] That they should seek the Lord, if haply they might feel after him, and find him, though he be not far from

every one of us:

The perceptive response is universal in the human condition. In other words God doesn't just speak to believers through sensing to feel He speaks to all men everywhere through this feeling. This is what the Gospel of John refers to in the following verse:

> [John 1:9 KJV] [That] was the true Light, which lighteth every man that cometh into the world.

When you received Christ you did so at some level because you felt the conviction of the Holy Spirit and knew you needed to give your life to Christ.

The level of hearing that is described as knowing in your knower comes quite often as a deep feeling that doesn't have anything to do with rationale or any other process.

When you are ministering in prophetic evangelism you will often see people you speak over be overcome with emotion not because of the persuasiveness of what you are saying, but because the Holy Spirit is working with you communicating with your target person through the PERCEPTIVE RESPONSE.

In Conclusion:

Receiving from God through the PERCEPTIVE RESPONSE is the most common way that God speaks not only to His children but to all men. The perceptive response runs quite deep in most men and women and will guide you in much the same way brute animals are guided by a bit in the mouth attached to reins in the hands of their riders.

The Holy Spirit will TUG on your heart and many times you will FEEL this in your body.

It can be very potent and strong but more often than not it is quite gentle so it is up to us to hear and respond without having to be "hit over the head with a board" to get it that God is speaking and we need to listen.

This Chapter's Activation Assignment:

This chapter's assignment is to minister again over a group of recipients (at least 5) that your group leader may choose or if you are working independently a list of your own. Remember you are practicing and this is intended to be a safe, learning environment.

So you are going to tune in to God and believe for a word for each recipient and then be willing to step out in faith to HEAR what God is saying. In the last chapter we exercised the ACOUSTIC RESPONSE but this week I want you to make the effort to SENSE in the Spirit what the Father says over each recipient.

CHAPTER EIGHT: MINISTERING FROM A PURE STREAM

Ministering From A Pure Stream

In the three previous chapters we introduced the primary modalities the Father speaks through. To review, they are:

> THE VISIONARY RESPONSE: Seeing what God is Saying
>
> THE ACOUSTIC RESPONSE: Hearing what God is Saying
>
> PERCEPTIVE RESPONSE: Feeling what God is Saying

God Is Always Speaking

The responses mentioned above deal with the modalities of spiritual hearing. Once you become fluent in these primary ways in which God speaks you will realize that you have in fact been hearing all along. God is always speaking we just aren't always listening.

> *[Amos 8:11] - 11 Behold, the days come, saith the Lord GOD, that I will send a famine in the land, not a famine of bread, nor a thirst for water, but of hearing the words of the LORD:*

Hearing from God is no great mystery and doesn't require some mystical lofty calling. This course is about making clear and concise communication with God easy and assessable. The suggestion that hearing from God requires living a mystical, or ascetic lifestyle assumes that the Father doesn't want to be heard and holds Himself aloof from His people. This is incorrect.

The Commission Of The Prophet

The *prophetic* is the term we use to refer to the act of hearing and articulating what the Father is saying in any given situation. The prophet is not the secret "keeper of the flame" of God's voice. The New Testament prophet is the discipler commissioned by God to assist you and train you to hear the Father's voice for yourself and articulate that voice for those you are responsible for.

> [Hebrews 1:1-3] - 1 God, who at sundry times and in divers manners spake in time past unto the fathers by the prophets, 2 Hath in these last days spoken unto us by [his] Son, whom he hath appointed heir of all things, by whom also he made the worlds; 3 Who being the brightness of [his] glory, and the express image of his person, and upholding all things by the word of his power, when he had by himself purged our sins, sat down on the right hand of the Majesty on high;

There is a difference between an Old Testament Prophet and a New Testament Prophet. The Old Testament Prophet was a primary source of inspiration whereas the New Testament prophet is the representative of Jesus Himself. Jesus Himself is the interpretive lens through which we filter everything we understand God to be saying in the earth today.

This is why it is inappropriate to "call fire down from heaven" or speak judgment and doom on someone claiming you are doing so by "prophetic inspiration".

> *[Luke 9:54-55] - 54 And when his disciples James and John saw [this], they said, Lord, wilt thou that we command fire to come down from heaven, and consume them, even as Elias did? 55 But he turned, and rebuked them, and said, Ye know not what manner of spirit ye are of.*

It is commonly taught today that a modern prophet has authority to do what Jesus forbade James and John to do. This is patent falsehood. ALL PROPHECY must be held to the litmus test of 1 Cor. 14:3 whether it is given by a seasoned prophet or by a baby Christian just venturing into the gifts of the Spirit.

> *[1 Corinthians 14:3] - 3 But he that prophesieth speaketh unto men [to] edification, and exhortation, and comfort.*

Many times you will hear judgmental people speak in harshness and a critical spirit. When they are asked to justify their actions they claim "That's just how I am ... I am prophetic that's my call." This is not true. You will not find one instance in the gospels or epistles of a New Testament prophet speaking in a harsh or judgmental tone.

A true prophet with a New Testament calling will speak in the Spirit of Christ with the love and compassion of the Father even to the most derelict human beings. This is a key to ministering from a pure stream. You have to lose your judgments, pet peeves, criticisms and high-mindedness if you are to used by the Father to minister the comfort of the Holy Ghost to others.

The Purpose Of The Prophetic Office Is To Teach Us To Hear

Paul makes the purpose of prophets and the other ministry Jesus gave very clear in Ephesians chapter four:

> [Ephesians 4:11-12] - 11 And he gave some, apostles; and some, prophets; and some, evangelists; and some, pastors and teachers; 12 For the perfecting of the saints, for the work of the ministry, for the edifying of the body of Christ:

It is possible that you will stand in the office of a prophet one day if you don't already. Your job is to hear God's voice and articulate it for the people. Your job is also to teach others how to be a prophetic people. Teaching others how to be a prophetic people is simply teaching them to hear God's voice for themselves and to articulate what they hear for the benefit of others.

Hearing, seeing, sensing what the Father says will come easier with time. Once you learn the basics you must now turn your attention to perfecting your hearing and perfecting your sharing. Without proper training you will not be able to share a pure stream and the greatest benefit will not be gained from those you share with.

Opinions Corrupt And Contaminate The Pure Stream Of God's Spirit

> [Matthew 7:1-2] - 1 Judge not, that ye be not judged. 2 For with what judgment ye judge, ye shall be judged: and with what measure ye mete, it shall be measured to you again.

The foregoing scripture is quite familiar to all of us but if you dig a little deeper you will see just how close to home it comes to our own heart and life. The word "judge" here means "to hand down an opinion". Opinions are lethal. Opinions cloud your judgment and rob you of the purity of true discernment. Opinions will negatively activate the law of reciprocity (sowing and reaping) in your life.

> [1 Corinthians 13:12] - 12 For now we see through a glass, darkly; but then face to face: now I know in part; but then shall I know even as also I am known.

The word "darkly" here means "in obscurity". We look to the Father and tune our ear to hear Him but often find our opinions and judgments are clouding what He is trying to say. There are many voices and many visions. As prophetic people we must learn how to quiet the internal dialog and hear just the Father's voice. There is no life in our opinions there is only life and anointing in voicing the Father's heart.

Tuning In To The Father's Voice – Tuning Out The "Many Voices"

> [1 Corinthians 14:10] - 10 There are, it may be, so many kinds of voices in the world, and none of them [is] without signification.

This was Adam and Eve's problem in the garden. They not only heard the voice of the Father walking in the cool of the day but they also heard the other voices. They had the authority to silence the serpent and you have the authority to silence OPINION in your life. Granted this is an area where lack of discipline is common but it is necessary to fine-tune your spiritual hearing.

This involves garnering maturity in your personal walk with God and developing familiarity with His voice on a day-to-day basis.

> *[Hebrews 5:14] - 14 But strong meat belongeth to them that are of full age, [even] those who by reason of use have their senses exercised to discern both good and evil.*

The above verse underscores why this course focuses on learning by doing. It is only through hearing and sharing what you sense the Father is saying that you begin to tell the difference between God's voice, your voice and the enemy's voice.

Working Through The Difficulties Of Hearing What God Is Saying

The greatest challenge of the prophetic is to give a pure word to someone you are familiar with and have emotional attachments to. On the one hand you have to filter through your own opinions and thoughts about this person and on the other hand you must set aside the lack of credibility you will have with those close to you:

> *[Mark 6:4] - 4 But Jesus said unto them, A prophet is not without honour, but in his own country, and among his own kin, and in his own house.*

With training it can become relatively easy for you to prophesy accurately to someone you know little or nothing about. Ministering to those not known to you is a great advantage because your perceptions are not obscured by personal knowledge of what is going on in that individual's life.

However the more you know the more of a challenge it is to set your own thoughts aside and prophesy the pure stream to the person before you. An even greater difficulty is prophesying to those close to you. Emotional attachments induce us to skew what we are saying one way or the other. With discipline you can set these emotional considerations aside and just hear and share what the Father is saying and nothing else.

Practice Having No Opinion

> *[Psalm 46:10 KJV] - 10 Be still, and know that I [am] God: I will be exalted among the heathen, I will be exalted in the earth.*

Losing your opinion is of great value in your walk with God. Have you noticed the continual stream of opinions that runs through your mind? The Psalmist speaks to this problem admonishing us to "BE STILL AND KNOW"... As you quiet the internal dialog of judgments and opinions the still small voice of the Father that is always speaking will surface within you.

A Personal Experience

One night I awoke in the early morning hours. Though it was still dark yet in the room I felt the tangible presence of God. I got up and lay on the floor at the foot of the bed. As I lay there the presence of God began to increase exponentially more and more. In response I began to pray in the Spirit in tongues. As I prayed in tongues however the presence of God began to withdraw and I heard the Father say in my spirit "Shhhh!" So I got quiet.

Once again in that silence the presence of God began to build and build upon me. I was shaking under the weight of the awesome presence of God. I began again to pray this time in English. To my puzzlement once again as I prayed the presence of God began to wane. Once more I heard the Father in my spirit "Shhhh!" So I got quiet once again.

Demystifying the Prophetic: Prophetic Activation Internship

As I lay there in silence the Father reminded me that I had been seeking to know what it was to "be still and know" that He was God. It had been quite a frustrating effort on my part. I had great difficulty quieting myself because my mind would race here and there the longer I stayed in my quiet place before the Father. This had gone on for months.

This night was different. The Father reached out and began to gently correct me. "You have an opinion about everything..." He chided me. "Learn not to have an opinion. Say within yourself in regard to matters great and small 'I have no opinion'." Then He spoke something to me that I've never forgotten:

"The Spirit of God is in the ascendancy when the mind and will of man is in abeyance. But the Spirit of God withdraws and recedes where the will of man and the mind of man are asserting themselves..."

If you want to see a magnification of the presence and glory of God in your life the key is to empty yourself of your own thoughts and viewpoints so you can receive the Father's pure heart and mind.

Thus instructed by the Father I embarked on a journey toward having no opinion. I would wake up in the morning and my mind would offer its opinion on the day. I would go to my place of business or some other activity and found my mind offering to form its opinion on every little thing. The Father had instructed me in my internal dialog to simply reply "I have no opinion about that ...." And voila! Suddenly the quietness of spirit I had longed for was manifest.

Through the discipline of the Father the sheer volume of my thoughts began to diminish and the state of internal quietness whereby the Father is more greatly known began to usher me in to an intimacy with the Father I had longed for.

There was a backlash though. My friends and acquaintances weren't too comfortable with the new quieter Russ Walden. My mother called my family and my brothers insisting that something was seriously wrong because I had gotten so quiet within. They would call me up and dish on some mutual friend and ask me what I thought. My response was "I have no opinion about that …." Over the course of time I actually lost friends because I would not run with them into areas of criticism gossip and opinion. The upside on the other hand was much greater clarity in hearing the Father's voice.

Moving Beyond Opinion Into The Mind Of God

[Isaiah 55:8] - 8 For my thoughts [are] not your thoughts, neither [are] your ways my ways, saith the LORD.

In choosing to have no opinion I placed myself in a position where the Father could speak to me beyond the level of my understanding. Until you relinquish your judgments you will never grow in wisdom in the things of God because you bind Him to only speaking to you in the vocabulary of your own reason.

> *[Jeremiah 31:34 KJV] - 34 And they shall teach no more every man his neighbour, and every man his brother, saying, Know the LORD: for they shall all know me, from the least of them unto the greatest of them, saith the LORD: for I will forgive their iniquity, and I will remember their sin no more.*

It is true that the Father will never speak to us contrary to His precious word. However He will frequently speak to us contrary to OUR FINITE UNDERSTANDING of His truth and His word.

Allow the Father to take you beyond your experience and learning into His limitless and unbiased mind.

In Conclusion

The pure stream of the mind of God flows through your heart as you set aside your finite understanding and allow His infinite wisdom to be expressed through you whether you understand or not. You will say many times "I'm not sure what this means but this is what I hear the Father saying..." Remember you are only the mail carrier. You can distance your mind and emotions from the prophetic by setting your opinions and passions aside.

> [Colossians 3:1] - 1 If ye then be risen with Christ, seek those things which are above, where Christ sitteth on the right hand of God.

When you prophesy you are reaching into the inventories of the glory in behalf of the person you are ministering to. Even if the person is a spouse or relative you can experience the release of the pure stream of the Spirit.

Now we invite you to go to the Prophetic Internship Response forum on Facebook and exercise the PERCEPTIVE RESPONSE in ministering to the recipients assigned to be ministered to this week.

This Chapter's Activation Assignment:

This chapter's assignment is to minister again over a group of recipients (at least 5) that your group leader may choose or if you are working independently a list of your own. Remember you are practicing and this is intended to be a safe, learning environment.

CHAPTER NINE: RIGHTLY DISCERNING WHAT YOU HEAR

Introduction:

In the previous few chapters we covered the visionary response, the acoustic response and the perceptive response as three primary modes through which the Father speaks. In this last chapter we taught on how to minister from a pure stream. Our opinions can and do enter in to the prophetic word when we share, but with diligence and humility we can set aside our thoughts and feelings and give the PURE word of the Father.

In this chapter we will turn our attention more acutely on distinguishing the origin of what you are hearing. The previous chapter dealt with sharing what the Father says without contaminating the word with your opinions. We will identify the origin of the voices you hear most often and how to tell the difference between YOUR VOICE, GOD'S VOICE, and most importantly how to identify and disregard the voice of the enemy.

Spiritual Hearing Is Perfected By Practice

Years ago I mentored a young man in the ministry for a period of time and in due course he asked me to appoint him to a place of responsibility. He said "I have a lot of mistakes to make before I get it right so go ahead and give me something to do..." What a great attitude! This is why in our prophetic internships we emphasis LEARNING BY DOING. You have a lot of mistakes to make so we give you a safe nurturing environment to practice until you also "GET IT RIGHT"!!!

> [Hebrews 5:14] - 14 But strong meat belongeth to them that are of full age, [even] those who by reason of use have their senses exercised to discern both good and evil.

The number one prerequisite for the prophetic is humility. I never argue with people who return back to me with a report that I had prophesied inaccurately. I rejoice in the fact that after prophesying for years to hundreds I am still a learner. I am still feeling after His voice and seeking to perfect my discernment of what the Father is saying. If you get frustrated or embarrassed then you have an indication that you need to work on some trust and acceptance issues between you and the Father.

Remember the Father loves you because he loves you. Just like our own children when they were toddlers we rejoiced in every little thing they did. When they faltered or made a mess of things they weren't making us mad, they were making a memory. The sweetest memories I have of my children as toddlers are instances where things were broken, spilled or stumbled over as they were learning how to navigate in this brand new world they were born to.

You and I have been born to the kingdom. We are going to break things, spill the milk, stumble and fail and the Father looks at the Son and smiles saying, "We are just making a memory!"

So relax and don't take yourself so seriously. You can never learn if you think someone (God or anyone else) is going to scream at you if you make a mistake.

Spiritual Hearing Comes To Us Through Intuition:

Spiritual hearing arises from the same capacity that produces what we call "intuition". It just so happens that ladies are by nature more gifted in this area than most men. We have all heard of "Mother's intuition" whereby Moms "just know" what they need to know about what's going on in their children's lives whether it is the fact that "Johnny stubbed his toe" or "Janie didn't really spent the night at her friend's house like she was supposed to..."

Where does this capacity for "knowing" arise from?

Intuition defined: *"Intuition is the power of guidance from a higher power. This is how some people seem to always know the right answer which comes to them trans-rationally not from any natural observation, learning or education."*

Intuition is the conduit between spiritual things and the mind and emotions. Sometimes intuition causes you to "just know" something. Other times it isn't a matter so much of knowing but rather an emotional reaction that isn't triggered by any outward event (like getting a good or bad feeling about a person place or thing for no apparent reason).

In view of the fact that intuition connects you to all things spiritual it is important to note that NOT EVERYTHING SPIRITUAL is godly or originating the Spirit of God.

When you are hearing and discerning you can legitimately ask yourself: "Is this MY spirit, GOD'S spirit or does this originate with our enemy the devil?"

As mentioned above ladies tend to INTUIT more often and more deeply than men do. Therefore it is not surprising that EVE was the first one to hear the voice of the serpent (See Gen. 3:1-6). Now theologians through the years have used the fact that Eve first heard the serpent as a basis for criticizing Eve as a part of the problem.

Even Adam himself when confronted by the Father blamed Eve:

> [Genesis 3:12 KJV] - 12 And the man said, The woman whom thou gavest [to be] with me, she gave me of the tree, and I did eat.

The fact that Eve heard the tempter first is not because she was more susceptible to evil but simply because God made women to be more intuitive. Women not only hear the voice of God readily they tend to hear all the voices whereas men quite often hear nothing at all.

Men who ignore this fact do so at their own peril such as Pilate's wife who in spite of being a pagan heard from God in a dream that her husband should have nothing to do with Jesus' condemnation and crucifixion.

> [Matthew 27:19 KJV] - 19 When he was set down on the judgment seat, his wife sent unto him, saying, Have thou nothing to do with that just man: for I have suffered many things this day in a dream because of him.

Developing Your Human Intuition As An Organ Of Spiritual Hearing:

Intuition can be suppressed and it can also be developed and enhanced. Many bible teachers will caution against this as an unsafe area of inquiry. But God made the human spirit to be an instrument through which He would lead guide and guard us, if we develop a hearing ear.

> [Proverbs 20:27 KJV] - 27 The spirit of man [is] the candle of the LORD, searching all the inward parts of the belly.

> *[1 Corinthians 2:11 KJV] - 11 For what man knoweth the things of a man, save the spirit of man which is in him? even so the things of God knoweth no man, but the Spirit of God.*

You need to learn to listen to the human spirit that God put on the inside of you. Your human spirit is the instrument by which God will communicate to you. It is also His dwelling place on the inside of you.

When you have questions your spirit will go to work on those problems taking up where your mind in its finite knowledge leaves off. Your human spirit never sleeps or slumbers. It always communicates with the Father and taps into His limitless knowledge pulling down answers for your life and lives of others.

Excluding The Voice Of The Enemy From What You Hear:

Identifying the voice of the enemy is easy no matter how cunning and deceptive he is. Let us remember that the devil is a finite being with limited knowledge and limited ability. He is NOT equal yet opposite to God. He has a finite number of strategies that can be learned identified and readily exposed if you simply choose not to be intimidated by the smoke and mirrors of the master deceiver.

The enemy's voice is almost always external to you. Paul taught us that the mystery of the Kingdom is "Christ in You the Hope of Glory" (Col. 1:25-28).

The enemy's voice appeals to your reason and your opinions. When he conversed with Eve he basically said over and again "it stands to reason…" The enemy appealed to Adam and Eve's rationale that it was ok and a good thing to disobey God. God hasn't called us to be led by human rationale or limited human logic or understanding.

The Father has called us not to partake of the TREE OF KNOWLEDGE (of good and evil) but to live by the TREE OF LIFE which originates in THE FATHER'S MIND and SPIRIT which communicates through our human spirit.

The enemy's voice speaks in vagaries and generalities. He speaks condemnation and judgment without clarity or specificity. He condemns YOU in your PERSON as well as highlighting your sins and failures. God's spirit on the other hand will always be quite specific.

> *[John 16:7-8] - 7 Nevertheless I tell you the truth; It is expedient for you that I go away: for if I go not away, the Comforter will not come unto you; but if I depart, I will send him unto you. 8 And when he is come, he will reprove the world of sin, and of righteousness, and of judgment:*

It has been said you will know a wolf by its tracks. When you hear something for yourself or for others ask yourself "does it measure up to the Spirit of Christ"?

> *[1 Corinthians 14:3 KJV] - 3 But he that prophesieth speaketh unto men [to] edification, and exhortation, and comfort.*

If what you are hearing isn't edifying or bringing exhortation and comfort then you can dismiss it. This doesn't mean that the Father never rebukes. Generally rebuke will come through the written word and those who are anointed to bring that word to us in counsel and teaching. But when you put a "thus saith the Lord" on something it is an ERROR to allow those words to come forth with judgment wrath and anger. This isn't a popular viewpoint but if you study the New Testament you will not find one instance of a PROPHET bringing judgment or wrath. In fact Jesus warned "you know not what spirit you are of" (See Luke 9:55).

The words of the enemy are not peaceable. Isa. 55:12 says that we will be "led forth with peace..." God's spirit will not lead through agitation, anger or anxiety. The Father will not use anything contrary to His character to guide or lead you in any way.

Eliminating Your Voice From What You Hear:

There is a secret mystical name for the Father I've learned over the years (speaking humorously now): That name is "SOMETHING". I told Kitty His name is "Jehovah-Something". How many times have you found yourself in situations where you had an "ah hah" moment and declared: "Something told me that was going to happen..." or "something told me that was the case..." etc., etc. The Father will never blow a trumpet or speak with grandiose fanfare. The voice of the Father is very often quiet and almost subliminal in character.

> [1 Kings 19:12 KJV] And after the earthquake a fire; [but] the LORD [was] not in the fire: and after the fire a still small voice.

Elijah's life was an uproarious and raucous adventure. Extraordinary miracles, signs and wonders were the norm for his every day experience. He needed a reminder of the deep things of God that speak in the very depths of quietness in your being. Therefore the Father sent fire, flood and earthquake Elijah's way but the spirit of God was only found in the still and small voice. When Elijah realized this he put a cloak over his face in awe of the still, small presence of God.

> [Deuteronomy 32:2 KJV] - 2 My doctrine shall drop as the rain, my speech shall distil as the dew, as the small rain upon the tender herb, and as the showers upon the grass:

When the prophet Moses heard from God the voice came in subtlety and gentleness. Just as moisture condenses imperceptibly on the outside of a glass of ice water so the voice of God just seems to have been there long before we realized it. Hence we conclude that God is always speaking but we aren't always listening.

Elijah learned that God didn't speak according to his own expectations. When you hear something that reinforces your own long-held concepts of God or your opinions about what God might think or say this is a time to get still and listen a little deeper than you normally do.

For myself I am quite cautious about asking a direct question to the Father because he ALWAYS defies my understanding and stretches me to my limit when I ask. The voice that expresses itself comfortably within the confines of our opinion, learning and experiences is quite often not the voice of the Father but the voice of human reasoning. Learn to expect the Father to speak outside the parameters of your understanding and background.

> [Isaiah 55:8 KJV] - 8 For my thoughts [are] not your thoughts, neither [are] your ways my ways, saith the LORD.

Clarifying The Father's Voice And Giving It Preimminence:

When you are listening for the Father's voice in your life or in behalf of others you must train yourself to give heed to the FIRST WITNESS that speaks. The first thing you hear is quite often the clearest most pure expression of what the Father is trying to show you. This may come quietly and so subliminally that you don't realize it at first.

Train Yourself Not To Overcomplicate Hearing From God:

You don't have to be an intellectual giant to hear the voice of the Father. In fact many of those who are greatly developed in their intellect have the most difficulty quieting the internal dialog and simply tuning in to the voice of the Father.

Learn to interact with the voice of the Father. I've heard prophets stop in front of crowds and ask the Father "could you say that one more time I wasn't listening close enough..." These prophetic ministers who fly in the face of religious convention are some of the most accurate and deep prophetic voices I know.

When you learn how to receive the Father's voice you will experience interference. It's as though you are tuned in to a radio station and have to adjust the dial to keep the signal clear. When I feel my mind crowding out what the Father is saying I transition into tongues when I am prophesying. This shuts my mind down and gives the reins of control back to the Holy Spirit.

To watch a prophet go through these seeming "antics" may seem like they are just being theatrical but in fact these are practical strategies to stay anchored in the voice of God in the moment at the time the answer is needed.

This Chapter's Activation Assignment:

The assignment in this chapter is to minister over a group of five BUT ALSO to minister and prophesy to someone OUTSIDE THE GROUP that is related to you by blood. The group of recipients (at least 5) will be chosen by your group leader or if you are working independently a list of your own. Remember you are practicing and this is intended to be a safe, learning environment.

CHAPTER TEN: PROPHETIC EVANGELISM: REACHING YOUR JERUSALEM

Demonstration and Prophetic Evangelism:

In the last chapter we stretched and challenged ourselves to speak and share prophetically with someone close to us. This may have been a family member or a close friend. This activation assignment was structured to move you out of the bracket of our internship group as a learning environment and to minister prophetically to someone close to you.

The preaching of the gospel is intrinsically prophetic in nature. We aren't called to tell others ABOUT Jesus! We are privileged rather to be the instruments by which Jesus DEMONSTRATES Himself in SPIRIT and in POWER. To merely talk ABOUT Jesus is just information. To DEMONSTRATE Jesus is TRANSFORMATION. The prophetic gifts that we are training for in this book are one way the Father will bring and introduce transformation through you to others. This lesson is about APPLYING the giftings of God. They aren't to be set on a shelf but used in everyday life.

The beginning place of sharing Christ is always those closest to you. It is true that prophetic people have very little respect from their friends and relatives:

> [John 4:44] 44 For Jesus himself testified, that a prophet hath no honor in his own country.

Nonetheless you shouldn't wait for perfect strangers to reach your loved ones. Jesus' entire ministry was to those related to him by blood. They were his family and his kinsmen. Jesus' kinsmen criticized him as you will be criticized. They brought up his past, his lack of credentials, etc. But Jesus remained undaunted. He persevered and church history tells us that later on many of his closest relatives were great leaders in the first century church. The relatives, spouse or sibling or cousins that oppose you the most will become your greatest allies when you refuse to be intimidated or daunted in bringing the presence of God to their door.

It isn't easy to share the DEMONSTRATION of the Spirit with loved ones but that is the starting place we are given in the scriptures:

> [Acts 1:8] But ye shall receive power, after that the Holy Ghost is come upon you: and ye shall be witnesses unto me both in Jerusalem, and in all Judaea, and in Samaria, and unto the uttermost part of the earth.

Your family is your Jerusalem. Your friends and neighbors are your Judea. The people in your community around you are your Samaria. The Holy Spirit and His gifts including the prophetic are the tools the Father gives you not to talk ABOUT but to DEMONSTRATE his active presence in the lives of those who don't know him as well as you do.

Demonstration And Prophetic Evangelism

The chapters in this book present the practical understanding of the prophetic gifts. We also cover the different applications of the prophetic. In this chapter we will consider prophetic as a tool of evangelism. Through the prophetic you circumvent the mental arguments and objections to the gospel and bring a person to a direct decision about the claims of Christ. Prophetic evangelism has been present in the church since the first century.

The last chapter was an appropriate preparation for the subject of prophetic evangelism. We studied the challenge of RIGHTLY DIVIDING AND DISCERNING THE VOICE YOU HEAR. When you are sharing Christ you will encounter many different people and situations. You have to be able to set aside your prejudices and opinions and ask yourself "Father what would you say to this individual?" It is possible with discipline and training to hear the Father's voice with clarity even in the most challenging situations.

Once you have heard the Father's voice you must then in obedience and humility share what He has communicated to you regarding the person in question. You must give what the Father gave you without needing to add to what He showed you or taking away from it. Even though you see, hear or sense something that may seem strange or out of place you have no idea what the Father has done to prepare that person to receive what you have to give. Be obedient. Don't second-guess the Holy Spirit's working.

> *[Mark 16:20] And they went forth, and preached every where, the Lord working with [them], and confirming the word with signs following. Amen.*

The Holy Spirit will go with you when He prompts you to share with your loved one, your neighbor or even a complete stranger. Prophetic evangelism is a potent ministry tools that will encourage and convince the most hardened individual.

Everyone Is Called To Prophetic Evangelism

When we use the "E" word (evangelism) the automatic response many times is "that is someone else's job I'm not called to evangelism".

Actually if you consider the "great commission" and what the disciples did with it you will find that those who did the greatest exploits of evangelism in the early church weren't even called to the fivefold ministry.

> [Mark 16:15-18] And he said unto them, Go ye into all the world, and preach the gospel to every creature. 16 He that believeth and is baptized shall be saved; but he that believeth not shall be damned. 17 And these signs shall follow them that believe; In my name shall they cast out devils; they shall speak with new tongues; 18 They shall take up serpents; and if they drink any deadly thing, it shall not hurt them; they shall lay hands on the sick, and they shall recover.

If you scrutinize the "Great Commission" passage above you will see it doesn't just speak to the apostles or the fivefold ministers. It speaks to "them that believe" (which includes every Christian). Every person who belongs to Christ is called to share the gospel or the good news about the love of God wherever they go. It doesn't require learning a "salvation plan" or some kind of religious sales pitch. It is not necessary to try to convince people that they need Jesus. The Holy Spirit that will go before you will convince and convict and cause the most self-sufficient, gospel resistant person to have a soft heart to receive His love.

Notice you are sharing the GOOD news. It isn't necessary to convince them they are sinners. You don't have to tell them they are going to hell. That isn't good news. People who aren't convinced in their own heart feel the need to manipulate and intimidate people trying to scare them into hell. People in the world already know the negatives. We are coming not to bring INFORMATION but the vital presence of God.

The Great Commission Is Intrinsically Prophetic

The "preaching" of the gospel doesn't require learning public speaking or the theological principles of leading someone to Jesus. The word preach here is the Greek word "*kerruso*" (sound familiar?). It describes the act of being a HERALD. A herald at the time Jesus said this was someone who ran ahead of a monarch and declared that "the King is coming..." Does this remind you of someone?

> *[Mark 1:7-8] And (John the Baptist) preached, saying, There cometh one mightier than I after me, the latchet of whose shoes I am not worthy to stoop down and unloose. 8 I indeed have baptized you with water: but he shall baptize you with the Holy Ghost.*

John the Baptist was the quintessential prophet. The Great Commission therefore is intrinsically prophetic. When you say the "king is coming" you may be referring in general to the "second coming" at the end of time but more specifically you are telling people that God is about to show up in their lives in a big way and you are there before them to articulate what that means and what blessing the Father is prepared to give them.

Examples From The Life Of The Early Church:

The gatherings of the early church were quite different from the meetings we attend week by week. We come into a building and sit obediently before a platform while a select group trained for that purpose lead us through worship and teaching. The activity of the modern church is primarily a spectator sport.

If we were to somehow get a raw look into the gathering of an early church assembly we would think it was some kind of chaotic free-for-all:

> *[1 Corinthians 14:26] How is it then, brethren? when ye come together, every one of you hath a psalm, hath a doctrine, hath a tongue, hath a revelation, hath an interpretation. Let all things be done unto edifying.*

Now the purpose of this lesson isn't to discuss early church structure. But we do want you to look at the above scripture and simply take note that the people who were a part of the early church were not observers or spectators. They were involved and actively participating in the meetings they were a part of.

Now if this was how they conducted themselves in their weekly gatherings is it not rational to deduce that this robust, prophetic and bold character was also demonstrated by them in their daily life in the public square? Consider the next scripture:

> [Acts 8:4] *Therefore they that were scattered abroad went every where preaching the word.*

Who are the "THEY" of this verse? They were not only the apostles and full time ministers. These were the rank and file every day Christians who were full of the power and presence of God. Whether they were in their weekly gatherings or at the work place or some other public venue they just wouldn't shut up.

As a believer you have the Spirit of God on the inside of you. He wants to use you. He wants to speak through you and further He wants to ACT through you. When Jesus speaks through you we call it prophesy and the DEMONSTRATION OF THE SPIRIT. When Jesus ACTS through you we call it the DEMONSTRATION OF POWER.

If you at times feel inadequate to share the truth of Jesus then simply submit to the spirit of prophecy and LET JESUS SPEAK FOR HIMSELF!

[Revelation 19:10] And I fell at his feet to worship him. And he said ... I am thy fellowservant, and of thy brethren that have the testimony of Jesus: worship God: for the testimony of Jesus is the spirit of prophecy.

How Effective Are The Prophetic Gifts In Convincing Unbelievers?

Have you ever shared Christ one on one with a loved one, a friend or complete stranger? It is challenging to be sure. If you were challenged by the prospect of sharing the simple salvation plan what is your reaction when I suggest that you can literally prophesy to these same people and not simply give them INFORMATION but DEMONSTRATION of the Spirit and Power?

You might be thinking "no way not me..." But first of all let's look at the impact of the prophetic on unbelievers. When Jesus stands up in your words and what you share you will find even the most stubborn people can have a dramatic and positive response. Consider the following verse:

> *[1 Corinthians 14:24-25] But if all prophesy, and there come in one that believeth not, or [one] unlearned, he is convinced of all, he is judged of all: 25 And thus are the secrets of his heart made manifest; and so falling down on [his] face he will worship God, and report that God is in you of a truth.*

How would you like to see the biggest sinner closest to you fall on their face and give glory to God. That's what this assignment is all about! Are you ready to start seeing results in sharing your faith? The verse above is not about giving mere information but rather sharing out of the gift of prophecy and allowing the Holy Spirit to take over and bring the person to Christ through the anointing He places on what you share and say.

You don't have to walk up to a stranger and shout "Thus saith the Lord..." That is religious thinking. You can go through a checkout line and say to the clerk "You know what I appreciate about you?" And see what God does, what comes out of your mouth next. The prophetic in an evangelistic setting is quite often conversational in its format. Just ask the Father to lead you.

The prophetic is not for the timid but I don't think you would have signed up for this course if you were at your core a timid little mouse. Let's be bold in this week's assignment and see what adventure the Father will lead you on.

This Weeks Activation Assignment: Prophetic Evangelism

Remember that you are to share the gospel to your personal Judea, Jerusalem, Samaria and all of the world. In the last chapter if you did the assignment you shared with someone close to you, a family member or dear friend.

This week your assignment is to prophesy is to a group of 5 recipients chosen by your group leader or by yourself and also to prophesy (hear from God and share what you hear) to a specifically to someone in your life that is more an acquaintance than a close friend who isn't related to you by blood.

This should be someone who knows you quite well but who you would call first before you went to visit or if they came to see you they wouldn't walk in without knocking. The last chapter was ministering to your *Jerusalem* – now you are going to share prophetically with someone in your *Judea*.

It doesn't matter whether they are born again or not. The good news is for everybody. Your born again best friend needs to hear the Father's voice and word for them as much as a lost person.

Prophesying to those close to you involves filtering out voices, opinions and judgments other than the Father's. You will hear many things on the inside of you when you ask the Father for encouragement for this target person for our assignment. Don't try to judge with 100% accuracy that this is "totally God". Just share with them the most loving positive thing that comes to you. Remember that God is love. You never go wrong letting love rule when you give words to another person. Remember this level of prophecy is important. The enemy is prophesying to people all the time (in their own thoughts). He is speaking doom and gloom and discouragement to people continually.

This is your opportunity to knock down the condemnation of the enemy and speak encouragement and comfort to your friend perhaps at a time when they need it most.

Now you are going to have to choose your target. You already know who it is. You don't have to think about it. Follow your first witness.

Don't second guess yourself and pick the easy one. Don't worry about making yourself convincing. Do what you can with what comes natural to you. It may be a simple word, a touch or a hug when they least expect it. Let love rule.

Don't hesitate in this. Be bold. You don't have to use any theatrics or "King James Thus Saith the Lord!". You can write what you feel down if you wish and hand it to them or you can deliver the word conversationally. You could just ask "can I pray for you" and then begin to pray prophetically over the person you are targeting. There are as many delivery methods in the prophetic as there are people.

Your assignment is also to also REPORT BACK. When you complete the assignment below and deliver what you have to your target person then give a brief one or two paragraph narrative of what you did and what the response was.

Purpose:

This activation is a continuation of broadening your prophetic training from the confines of this group of interns and get you out in the real world sharing what the Father gives you. The good news is to your closest loved ones, then your friends and out into the entire world. It is challenging but we don't want to leave our closest loved ones out of what God is doing in our lives. They may have as difficult a time receiving what you share as you do sharing it but the experience is invaluable as you learn to overcome timidity and seek in the midst of your human imperfection to be an instrument of encouragement to others.

CHAPTER ELVEN: PUBLIC PROPHETIC DEMONSTRATION

In the last cahpter we introduced the prophetic as a tool of evangelism. In chapter nine I assigned you to prophesy to someone close to you (your Jerusalem); in week ten I had you prophesy to a friend or acquaintance not related to you by blood (your Judea). Are you ready to get a little bolder? This week your assignment is to PROPHESY IN THE MARKETPLACE, in other words you are to go out in public, where you work, where you shop or go to school and ask the Lord to give you a word of PROPHETIC EVANGELISM for someone you don't know.

We recommend that you review the previous chapter to refresh you and arm you for this exciting exercise. Let me give you an encouragement - this lesson is always the favorite of the interns after they come back and report the powerful way that the Father moves in this assignment. Is your heart racing? Did you say, "I'm not going do THAT!???" Sure you are. You didn't get into this to take the safe route. It's time to charge hell with a water pistol!

Now you don't go out to the Wal-Mart and shout "THUS SAITH THE LORD". Your assignment is to go out in your day and find that person that the Father points out to you. Then you start conversationally. Example from my own experience: I prophesied to the checker at Wal-Mart the other day. The Father showed me some obvious things about her and I opened my mouth and started with:

"Do you know what I appreciate about you?"

I went forward and ministered to her in the time it took to pay for my groceries. It will work just like that for you. Now get out there and DO THE STUFF! Then report to your class or group what you did, where you went, who you talked to and what the results were.

THIS IS WHERE THE FUN STARTS!!!!

This Is The Time To Be Bold, Experience Your Accuracy And Learn To Live With Your Mistakes:

For those that started with week one in this twelve-week rotation, this lesson is one of two final lessons. For those just starting out, just hang in there and week one will start after next week when the concluding lesson of the twelve-week rotation. Those who are new are welcome to skip this lesson if you wish and go to your e-mail and start with week one or the earlier lessons you have been working on. These lessons are designed to be helpful and useful for everyone no matter where you start in the twelve-week rotation.

I want to give you a few verses to consider about the prophetic in this lesson that deal with accuracy issues and what happens when you miss it. If you are going to move in the prophetic you must be willing to step out there and make a mistake a time or to. I remember one brother making the statement with a wry smile on his face: "I know I can miss it and I KNOW I can miss it..."

Here is an example of a reputable prophet who seriously "missed it": I saw one of the most prolific and anointed prophets I know prophesy for twenty minutes to a man about his life, about a woman that the Father had for him, about being a "father to fathers" etc., etc. As it turned out the "man" he was prophesying to was actually a WOMAN with some gender issues.

The prophet's wife in exasperation and embarrassment for her husband stopped him in the middle of his prophecy to him (actually her) and said, "Ira ... HE is a HER!" Ira hesitated a moment and made a few adjustments and finished prophesying to the person in question. Now did Prophet Ira miss it? Actually that isn't the point. In truth he simply illustrated what the Bible teaches about the prophetic:

> *(1 Corinthians 13:8-12 KJV) - Charity never faileth: but whether [there be] prophecies, they shall fail... For now we see through a glass, darkly; but then face to face: now I know in part; but then shall I know even as also I am known.*

I don't care how long you have been at this or what stature you rise to in the prophetic, you will still be operating on the principles described in the passage above:

1. Prophecies will fail

2. We know in part and prophesy in part

3. We see through a glass darkly

Now let me challenge you. Even JESUS HIMSELF gave a prophecy that didn't come to pass and never will come to pass. (Gasp!) Read the following scripture:

> *(Matthew 19:28 KJV) - And Jesus said unto them, Verily I say unto you, That ye which have followed me, in the regeneration when the Son of man shall sit in the throne of his glory, ye also shall sit upon twelve thrones, judging the twelve tribes of Israel.*

Now when you read the passage above you will see that Jesus is speaking to his twelve disciples. One of those disciples was JUDAS! And the prophecy Jesus is making in the verse above didn't come to pass in Judas' life and never will. You can make all kinds of rationalizations about this but in fact this word AS GIVEN to WHOM IT was given did not fully come to pass and never will. What can we learn from this?

For one thing, prophecies are CONDITIONAL.

If you are bold in the prophetic you will have people come back and say, "that word you gave me didn't come to pass..." But there are a few questions to ask yourself about that. Did you fail in the prophetic or was there a CONDITION that the person receiving the prophecy failed to fulfill?

Example from my own ministry:

I gave a prophesy to a man that within 90 days his employment situation and his relationship issue would be resolved by the hand of God. Many weeks later I got a phone call at 5 a.m. (I hadn't even had my first cup of coffee!).

It was "Ted" on the other line. He launched right in, railing on me that I was unsafe, that he should have never submitted to me for prophecy, that prophets who put time frames on prophetic words were patently false, etc., etc. I stood there listening, sipping my coffee, and watching the sun come up out my window. Then I turned and checked the calendar. I saw that the 90-day time frame the Father gave me for him hadn't expired yet. There were yet two more days to wait! There were two more days for the prophecy to come to pass!

I pointed out the two remaining days to Ted and told him to call me back and finish chewing me out after the 90 days God gave me for him had actually expired. Guess what happened? That's right, within two days he had a job offer (after 5 years of being unemployed and homeless) and he renewed a relationship with a prospective fiancée.

What does that teach you? That I was actually "God's man of faith and power"? No, that isn't the point. The point is that the prophetic is never black and white and the edges of clarity in the prophetic are seldom sharp and clear. You cannot get discouraged if you make a mistake. You don't always know and even the person you are prophesying to doesn't always have all the facts.

The prophetic gifts are about FLUENCY and EXPERIENCE. You get better at the prophetic the more you prophesy and the more you move in the gifts of God. You have to learn this. Other issues in the prophetic reflect people wanting to use the prophetic for more than it is intended for. We are not fortunetellers. We are not palm readers or astrologers.

> *(Isaiah 8:19 KJV) - And when they shall say unto you, Seek unto them that have familiar spirits, and unto wizards that peep, and that mutter: should not a people seek unto their God? for the living to the dead?*

I personally love it when someone requests prophetic ministry and gives five or six very specific questions. Something about that makes my belly leap for joy and God gives me the answers they seek and I've never been told I missed it or was wrong. But there are other times the questions arise out of unbelief and pessimism. You will sense it when the occasion arises and you shouldn't hesitate to state flatly that you aren't a "new ager" or a palm reader.

Just because someone asks ONE thing doesn't mean you prophesy to him or her on HIS OR HER TERMS. We have had people ask us to tell us if their dead relative was still mad at them about this or that. Or we have people ask if the person they love is going to leave their spouse and marry them. When that happens we don't rebuke them out of hand. We LISTEN TO THE FATHER and then simply overlook their carnal or even sinful requests and minister straight to their hearts. We've seen individuals in these situations turn and give their heart to Christ in these situations.

As a prophet you will see many things that will disgust you and that you will find revolting in the people you minister to. It isn't your place to rebuke and castigate them. They know they are sinners, they know they are unclean. What they don't know is that God loves them. You have to minister out of the love of God, dealing with them according to their need not according to their problem. In so doing you launch the power of "Love never fails" in your prophetic ministry and will see great results.

How do you prophesy to people in public? The same way you do in this internship. Be confident. Be casual. Be loving and kind. Know that God is with you to confirm your words with His power even if you are rebuffed. Let the Lord lead you as you step out INTO THE WILD and exercise your gift. Be sure to come back to the internship form and share with the internship about how the Father used you and what the result was.

This Chapter's Activation Assignment:

The assignment in this chapter is to minister over a group of five BUT ALSO to minister and prophesy to someone OUTSIDE THE GROUP that is COMPLETELY UNKNOWN to you. The group of recipients (at least 5) will be chosen by your group leader or if you are working independently a list of your own.

CHAPTER TWELVE: MENTORING IN THE PROPHETIC

In the last chapter we advanced further the challenge of using the prophetic as a tool of evangelism. The assignment was to "go out into the wild" in public (where you work, shop, etc.) and to PROPHESY (conversationally or otherwise) to someone you didn't know.

We trust that you ALL SURVIVED and that you ALL MADE THE ATTEMPT. "Pulse pounding, heart racing" Christianity is so much fun. In this course we purpose to challenge you at every level. If you perhaps planned to "audit" this course you are going to be quite bored and it won't help you much. Each installment included a lesson and an assignment. The lessons are informational and inspirational. The assignments and activations are where the real learning and excitement begins.

For your information we are about to begin (starting next week) again with lesson one. Many of you dropped in the rotation at Lesson Six, Ten or whatever. You simply need to stay in the rotation and continue the weekly assignments and lessons to get the weekly installments that came before you started. For those of you finishing up this week you are welcome to continue but you do need to let us know so we don't take your name off the roster.

ACTIVATION - MENTORING IN THE PROPHETIC

In order to progress in the gifting of God for your life you have to share what you have. The exciting thing about the prophetic is showing those you love and those who are near to you that they can hear the Father's voice with clarity. The prophetic office and gifting isn't just about "going to get a word..."

It would be quite sad if the prophetic only served to make you dependent on hearing the word of the Lord from a prophet. Paul said in

Col. 1:27 that "Christ in YOU" is the hope of glory for your life. All true and mature ministers and prophets will always point you NOT TO THEMSELVES but to the CHRIST that dwells on the inside of you.

That being the case you (as a prophetic person) will have opportunities not only to prophesy to others but to also HELP OTHERS KNOW they are in fact hearing the voice of the Father for themselves.

So the final activation and assignment of our Prophetic Activation Internship is for you to reach out to a friend, a loved one or someone the Father leads you to - - and lead them in a simple activation. You can do this ONE ON ONE or perhaps you want to gather a small group together for a special time of sharing on what you learned in this course. The point of the assignment is for you to prophesy to that person(s) but also to show that person (or group) that they too can move in the prophetic and hear the voice of the Father with assurance and clarity.

EXAMPLE: KITTY'S SIMPLEST PROPHETIC ACTIVATION:

My wife Kitty have mentored others in the prophetic for many years. She taught Advanced Prophetic Training and certainly has mentored me greatly in the hearing of God's voice and sharing what I have heard. I owe her a great deal in that regard.

Kitty often does a simple activation that is one of my personal favorites:

You broach the subject of "hearing the voice of God" with a person or group. You may or may not share a set of scriptures or perhaps some helpful points from one of your favorite lessons in this course (you have our permission).

After some discussion (usually someone unfamiliar with the prophetic will say to you that they never hear God very clearly but they would like to). Then you ask them if they want to know RIGHT AT THAT MOMENT what it is like to hear God's voice clearly. They will no doubt say "yes".

Ask them to close their eyes.

Ask them to say their name silently to themselves.

After a moment inquire "did you hear your name when you said it silently?"

You tell them - "that's how easy it is to hear from God."

Be sure to report back to us what your experience was in doing this assignment.

The purpose of this simple activation is to point out to the person you are working with that the actual human ability to "inwardly ponder" or carry on an "inward dialogue" with oneself is the SAME CAPACITY that God uses to inject HIS THOUGHTS into YOUR THOUGHTS.

There are many ways God speaks but this is one of the most familiar and simplest ways to know the Father's voice. He uses the INSTRUMENTALITY of the internal dialogue that is on-going within people everywhere all the time.

FURTHER INSTRUCTION AND LEARNING HOW TO MENTOR IN THE PROPHETIC

If you continue to develop your ear for the voice of the Father you will have many opportunities to your prophetic gifting. It is important that you share out of your own experience. Tell what you KNOW and what you have seen and heard in your own adventure with the voice of the Father.

1. Share with them things you have learned about hearing the voice of God.

2. Then lead that person through a simple activation in hearing the

voice of God for themselves.

YOU DON'T HAVE TO BE A PROPHET TO "BE" PROPHETIC:

We decided to do this training because we see our responsibility not only to BE PROPHETIC ourselves but to train you as in the prophetic gifting. You may or may not be a prophet, but every believer is prophetic to some degree because the simplicity of the prophetic is found in hearing the Father's voice and articulating it for yourself and others.

In the medical community when an intern is learning medicine the principal by which they learn is:

1. Watch one 2. Do one 3. Teach one

This is our approach as well. You have watched others move in the gift of prophecy. You have observed how the prophetic gifting flows through anointing prophets. It is important to know that the "kingdom doesn't come with observation". Just watching the prophetic work doesn't bring the greatest blessing. The five-fold ministry is in place to teach you to do the work of the ministry that you have watched others do.

> *(Ephesians 4:11-12 KJV) - And he gave some, apostles; and some, prophets; and some, evangelists; and some, pastors and teachers; For the perfecting of the saints, for the work of the ministry, for the edifying of the body of Christ:*

If we are called to the five-fold ministry of the prophetic our job is not just to demonstrate the prophetic but to train you as well. Our job is to work ourselves out of a job by training you to do the work of the ministry that has been traditionally relegated to the 'professional clergy'. The 'clergy / laity' dichotomy is something that God hates because it fosters and validates lethargy in the body of Christ (See Rev. 2:6).

This is why each lesson has included a challenging activation exercise. If you haven't acted on each activation, then you haven't gotten much from this course because the kingdom doesn't come with observation. The kingdom of God is a PRESENT PARTICIPATION and as you have participated you have been ACTIVATED.

(Luke 17:20 KJV) - And when he was demanded of the Pharisees, when the kingdom of God should come, he answered them and said, The kingdom of God cometh not with observation:

SPIRITUAL GIFTS MUST BE CULTIVATED AND EXERCISED

Spiritual Gifts (including prophecy) don't just drop down on you without preamble or preparation. Consider the following verse:

> (1 Corinthians 12:31 KJV) - But covet earnestly the best gifts...

If you study the phrase "covet earnestly" it comes for the same word where we get the word 'zealous'. It includes the thought of STRIVING AFTER and EARNESTLY IMITATING and CULTIVATING the gifts of the spirit. This admonition is for every one whether you consider yourself a 'prophet' or not.

> (1 Corinthians 14:31 KJV) - For ye may all prophesy one by one, that all may learn, and all may be comforted.

As you continue to challenge yourself in the prophetic you will gain FLUENCY in the prophetic gift. The only way you can become more active and accurate is by stepping out there and prophesying, and honing your spiritual senses to hear His voice with greater and greater clarity.

(Hebrews 5:14 KJV) - But strong meat belongeth to them that are of full age, [even] those who by reason of use have their senses exercised to discern both good and evil.

SHARING THE PROPHETIC

There are many negative stereotypes of prophetic ministry that you will face as you exercise the gifting of God in your life. It is important to stay sweet in your soul and helpful in your approach in ministering to others.

You may feel that you are called not only to be prophetic but also to the OFFICE OF A PROPHET "ministry gift" of the prophetic or a "five-fold minister"). If so you want to consider a few things:

Once you finish this internship you might want to:

Start a Prophetic Small Group:

You could print out the e-mails you have received in this course and teach directly from them, or develop lessons yourself.

Hosting a Prophetic Encouragement Event:

You could host a Prophetic Encouragement Event in your community and invite a seasoned prophetic ministry to come and introduce the prophetic. Kitty and I are open to doing this very thing with those who have experienced the internship program.

Important things to remember:

Prophesy is for edification, exhortation and comfort. (See 1 Cor. 14:1-3). People need to know the love of God and his care for them. Prophecy is so powerful that God doesn't want us to use it for rebuke or correction. There are times rebuke is needed but the prophetic voice is never the gifting used to deliver a correction. Hiding behind 'thus saith the Lord' and rebuking someone is cowardice and gross misrepresentation of the prophetic gifting.

Always ask "may I prophesy to you?" Give the recipients you are ministering to a gracious opportunity to say, "thanks but no thanks". Don't get offended. It isn't about you, it is about Him and the Holy Spirit is always a "gentleman".

Prophesy is not a novelty, it is a core element in spiritual life and growth. Memorize 2 Chron. 20:20:

> *(2 Chronicles 20:20 KJV) - Believe in the LORD your God, so shall ye be established; believe his prophets, so shall ye prosper.*

Many people have believed in the Lord and received Jesus as savior. But they are living lives of quiet desperation and stagnation because they haven't received the further understanding of 'believe his prophets so shall ye prosper.'

As a prophetic voice your gifting is intended to bring people to breakthrough and victory in difficult areas of their life. The impact of your prophetic gifting on those you minister to is seen in the definition of the word 'prosper' from 2 Chron. 20:20:

Prosper: tsalach - to advance, prosper, succeed, to experience prosperity.

Many in the body of Christ are ESTABLISHED by believing in the Lord but they are not PROSPERING. That is the very definition of stagnation. God wants them to be established by believing in the Lord but to go further and prosper by believing in the prophetic gifting that he brings to them from time to time.

Remember: The prophetic gifting is all about HEARING THE VOICE OF THE FATHER and ACTIVATING OTHERS TO HEAR HIS VOICE FOR THEMSELVES.

THE PREREQUISITE OF HUMILITY

When you prophesy to others, or mentor others in the prophetic, always remember that you are SPEAKING TO THE CHRIST IN THEM. Kitty and I preface our ministry to each person with 'It is our privilege to speak to the Christ in you...' John the Baptist is our example. John the Baptist (who did no miracle - see John 10:41) was used by God to ACTIVATE JESUS IN HIS MIRACLE MINISTRY. John when he saw Jesus

declared:

> (John 1:29 KJV) - The next day John seeth Jesus coming unto him, and saith, Behold the Lamb of God, which taketh away the sin of the world.

John knew he wasn't worthy to speak to the Christ he saw in Jesus. Likewise you should adopt the same attitude of humility to those you minister to. You should always see the Lamb in them and speak over them with grace and humility knowing you are touching the apple of God's eye.

CONCLUSION:

Remember that material isn't about pride, or performance or learning something so you can do what others can't. This course is about activating you in a service of humility to set captives free and activate the voice of the Father in those who are longing to know Him more deeply.

Now you may go ahead and plan on fulfilling the assignment of sharing the prophetic gifting and an activating with an individual or a group. That is your final assignment. Be sure to respond back to your group with a report of how things progressed.

Made in the USA
San Bernardino, CA
15 October 2018